The Making of Blind Men
A Study of Adult Socialization

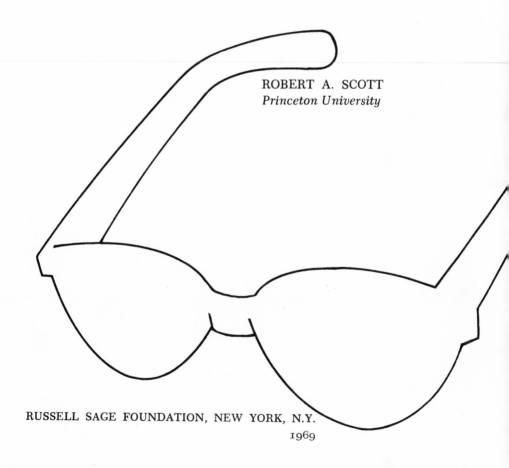

ROBERT A. SCOTT
Princeton University

RUSSELL SAGE FOUNDATION, NEW YORK, N.Y.
1969

To my father

FOREWORD

PERUSAL OF the literature in the field of services to blind and visually-impaired persons will yield no book more intensive or bound to
be more controversial than this. I believe that Dr. Scott's sensitive
negativism of the work being carried out by the so-called blind
agencies is emphasized for effect—hopefully, upon the officers and
administrative and supervisory staffs of all agencies, public and
private, large and small, specialized or multi-faceted. A critical
open-minded review of this book by those who are responsible for
the quality of services to blind persons today will leave no one guilt
free. The pertinent questions posed by Dr. Scott's observations require serious evaluation by each of us. In view of the sociological
system of *making* blind men (can one categorically deny it?), these
questions must be asked by each agency: "How have we actually contributed to this system?" "How do we see it affecting our
future role?"

I earnestly hope that the thinking members from the field and
the academicians will look at this book through the eyes of a social
scientist whose objective was to shock "blind agencies" out of their
lethargic, accommodative approaches and toward a new outlook for
brighter, clearer, and more realistic services for the blind. Throughout this nation and Canada there is a new emphasis upon sound,
responsible programs of multiple services geared to meet the re-
quirements of each blind individual for the maximum development
of his talents and desired objectives as an independent person
in society.

This new focus upon the development of the individual has required responsible persons in some agencies to seek the talents and experiences of professionally trained people who have, as their major objective in life, service to their fellow men.

More and more questions are being raised within the field of services to blind persons: "What can we do to build upon the past?" "How can we more effectively help each individual blind person by providing more quality services for his individual good?" In some agencies there is already a movement away from the status quo, one which holds great promise for the future of blind and visually-impaired persons. Through their example, change for the betterment of service, not complacency with the "old," is now in vogue. The continuing development of new approaches to service, new systems, skills, and techniques, which are based upon applied and clinical research, will dispel the bleak picture portrayed in this sophisticated text.

Those who have been concerned with other fields of serving handicapped persons can readily see that the observations and conclusions of Dr. Scott are not unique to the field of blindness. Nevertheless, it is important that we capitalize upon his critical review in order that we recognize the "individual differences" among the blind and visually-impaired persons, and gear our services, individually and collectively, to meet their needs. There has been a long-standing need for a treatise such as this, which is a most natural collateral to the self-evaluation guides produced by the National Accreditation Council for Agencies Serving Blind and Visually-Handicapped Persons. This book should produce one of the most thought-provoking, self-analytical exercises yet known to our field. Therefore, its contribution may be not only the thoughts that it contains, but also the thoughts that it provokes.

WESLEY D. SPRAGUE

New York City
October, 1968

PREFACE

IT IS with a special sense of personal satisfaction that I welcome
this addition to Russell Sage Foundation publications. During part
of the time that the author, Dr. Robert A. Scott, was engaged in his
research, he was a resident study director in the offices of the Foundation, and so I was able to see this work grow, take shape, come
to maturity, and to appreciate the ways in which the author moved
to solve the unusual practical and intellectual challenges of
the research.

   William M. Robbins, President of the Board of Trustees of the
New York Association for the Blind, and the late Alan W. Sherman,
then Executive Director of the Association, asked Russell Sage
Foundation to participate in a jointly-sponsored study of current
services for the blind in the United States, with special reference to
the contributions the social sciences might make in understanding
and improving the services. It was understood that the Association
would be an important, but not the only, major institution providing
services for the blind that would come under review, and that the
conclusions of the proposed study would certainly be useful to those
responsible for the program at the Association in planning new
ventures. The foresight and initiative demonstrated by Mr. Robbins
and Mr. Sherman in conceiving the study was equaled by the Association's exceptional candor and cooperation throughout the course
of the study.

In other years, Russell Sage Foundation has supported similar studies in cooperation with the Jewish Family Service, the Family Service Association of America, the Child Welfare League of America, the Child Study Association of America, and other major health and welfare organizations. These studies were directed toward improving the utilization of social science theory and knowledge in the day-to-day operations of these institutions. Accordingly, the Foundation welcomed the opportunity to work with the New York Association for the Blind in the important area of services for the blind. Both sponsoring parties were happy to avail themselves of Dr. Scott's services to direct this study.

This study is a powerful case analysis of a major human disability, of a set of welfare institutions designed to meet this disability. It also presents basic social science information that can be brought to bear on understanding the disability and the institutions' procedures. The key to Dr. Scott's study is given at the outset:

The disability of blindness is a learned social role. The various attitudes and patterns of behavior that characterize people who are blind are not inherent in their condition but, rather, are acquired through ordinary processes of social learning.

This basic sociological insight is developed in subsequent chapters. Dr. Scott has presented here an astute and terse layout of the basic theory of socialization and role-learning among human beings, with special reference to its application to learning to be blind, that is, learning the role assigned to a blind person. The data documenting the gross inequities in the organizations' selection of clients from among the possible population of clients, make it clear that some groups, such as children, are substantially favored over other groups, e.g., the aged.

Analysis of the interaction between the person and the social organization, in this case the client and the institution serving the blind, shows how the character of the organization works to create, through role definition, what we know today as the blind person. Organizations serving the blind are constrained in large part to operate the way they do because of the larger context of the nation's services for the blind. Competition for clients among the too-numerous blind-serving agencies, the character of the professional and quasi-professional service groups involved must be understood and dealt with in any effort on the part of a given agency to alter its program in client selection and in the roles assigned to the blind client.

Dr. Scott, by virtue of his analysis, shows the influential role that these institutions have in shaping the character of the blind person in the United States, and it is just this demonstration of influence that constitutes the basis for optimism about the future and justifies the challenge he gives to institutions. Any group of welfare institutions as powerful as this is with reference to its clients has a great opportunity for being effective in any new programs it undertakes.

ORVILLE G. BRIM, JR.

RUSSELL SAGE FOUNDATION
New York City
November, 1968

ACKNOWLEDGEMENTS

THIS STUDY was jointly sponsored by the New York Association for the Blind and by Russell Sage Foundation. I owe a major debt of gratitude to each of these organizations, and one that goes far beyond their financial support of this study. Board and staff members of The Lighthouse gave me their full and wholehearted cooperation throughout all phases of the project. They made every effort to provide me with the information I needed, and they helped me gain entree into many organizations and programs for the blind throughout the country. There are several persons at The Lighthouse to whom I am especially indebted. They are Saul Freedman, William F. Gallagher, and Marion Held of the staff; and William M. Robbins, who was President of the Board of Trustees at the time that this study was initiated. I also want to thank Wesley D. Sprague, Executive Director of The Lighthouse, for all of the assistance he gave me on this study. It was during the many conversations we shared together that I first began to appreciate the obstacles that stand in the way of implementing abstract ideals with concrete social actions; and it was from the many opportunities he gave me to observe at first hand the day-to-day activities of an agency director that I got a first-class object lesson in how to begin to circumvent some of these obstacles effectively. It is fair to say that, without his cooperation, support, and experience, this study could not have been completed. Finally, I want to acknowledge the foresight of the Trustees and executive officers of The Lighthouse in supporting a research project of this type.

I am equally indebted to the Trustees of Russell Sage Foundation for their financial support of this research, and to the staff for the excellent advice they gave me on all aspects of the project. The broad and unusual perspective they are able to bring to questions of the sort raised in this study indicates, I believe, the extreme importance of the Foundation's work for contemporary social science. I especially want to thank Orville G. Brim, Jr., President of Russell Sage Foundation, for the assistance he has given me throughout the study, and particularly for his excellent suggestions on various drafts of this manuscript.

There are others to whom I owe a great deal. Father Thomas J. Carroll, Milton D. Graham, and Hector Chevigny each gave me many days of his time, imparting to me the full value of his experiences with and ideas about blindness and work for the blind. Bruce D. Bassoff was indispensable as a research assistant and editor, as was Christine Valibus, who served as my secretary for two years. I also want to thank Leslie L. Clark, Eric Josephson, Robert L. Robinson, Hope J. Leichter, and Donald A. Schon for the advice and assistance they so ably gave me. While I have borrowed many of these ideas, I, of course, am solely responsible for the materials that are set forth in this book. I also wish to acknowledge Princeton University's support during the final year of this study. Finally, I am particularly grateful to Nancy and Michael for their patience as I struggled with the thorny problems of research and writing.

ROBERT A. SCOTT

Princeton, New Jersey
October, 1968

TABLE OF CONTENTS

INTRODUCTION

IN THE last hundred and fifty years, there has been developing in this country an increasingly formalized interest in helping blind people to participate more fully in the economic, social, and cultural life of the society. From relatively modest beginnings, this interest has evolved into a large, intricate, multimillion-dollar national network of organizations, professional specialities, and programs for blind people. The phrase "work for the blind" is used to designate this enterprise.

The first programs for the blind grew out of the intellectual interests and humanitarian concerns of a handful of people who were at once fascinated by the idea of attempting to educate children who could not see and horrified by the inhuman treatment often accorded them by their society. Later, privately sponsored local programs for the adult blind were established by various individuals and groups in order to meet what they perceived to be the most important and urgent needs of those in their communities who were blind. At the same time, the federal government and various state governments began to establish programs to meet specific needs of particular groups of blind people. It was through the tenacity and enterprise of many dedicated people that these various individual undertakings grew into the large network of public and private organizations, programs, and agencies that today offer services to people who are blind.

During these years, no systematic studies have been made of the effects this complicated network has had upon the blind people who come into contact with it, or on the broader social and welfare problems of blindness in our society. Most blindness workers have found themselves preoccupied (and understandably so) with other, more immediate problems in the day-to-day operations of the organizations and agencies for which they work. Moreover, while many people in work for the blind have expressed a keen interest in having research conducted on the effectiveness of service programs, there has been some reluctance to allocate the necessary funds because of a concern that the diversion might deprive blind people of badly needed services. Increasingly, however, blindness workers have come to regard the conduct of such research as a matter of some urgency. They recognize that work for the blind is no longer a small social-service enterprise. Today, the 800 or so separate organizations, agencies, and programs for the blind in America spend nearly $470,000,000 annually, and there is every indication that this enterprise will continue to grow and expand in the years to come. Many blindness workers are skeptical that the goals of so massive an enterprise will ever be achieved so long as there continues to be a data vacuum regarding both the scope of the blindness problem in our society and the impact upon that problem of the intervention programs of work for the blind. The project upon which this book is based grew out of a determination by various individuals and organizations in both the blindness field and the social sciences to begin to eliminate this vacuum.

As the project was originally conceived, its basic purposes were as follows: (1) to obtain a systematic and integrated overview of the blindness problem in America; (2) to determine which aspects of this problem are being dealt with by work for the blind and which are not; (3) to determine the effectiveness of this organized intervention system in dealing with the aspects of the blindness problem on which it focuses; (4) to determine the consequences for blind people of their becoming clients of blindness agencies; and (5) to determine the potential application of social science knowledge to the theory and practice of this field. In order to accomplish these objectives, I began to search for relevant data that already existed, with the idea of supplementing it where necessary with new information to be obtained through small, independent research studies. A thorough review of the literature and of other sources produced only a few reliable studies on any of the myriad aspects of blindness and work for the blind. It therefore fell to me to go out and collect whatever data could practicably be obtained, given the time and money constraints of the project. This search for data took me into the field, where I had an opportunity to speak at length with blind people from all walks of life and to become familiar with the day-to-day practices of workers in agencies that serve the blind. Two facts of paramount sociological importance emerged from these experiences. The first is that many of the attitudes, behavior patterns, and qualities of character that have long been assumed to be given to blind people by their condition are, in fact, the result of ordinary processes of socialization. The second is that organized intervention programs for the blind play a major role in determining the nature of this socialization. Blindness, then, is a social role that people who have serious difficulty seeing or who cannot see at all must learn how to play. This is the basic thesis of this book. I have not ignored the other questions I had originally set out to answer; rather, my answers to them are given in the context of documenting and explaining this basic thesis.

PAST EXPLANATIONS

Before explaining how the data of this study were obtained, I want to consider briefly some of the other major explanations that have been proposed for the attitudes and behavior patterns of the blind, and to indicate why I believe that they are inadequate. Three such explanations can be identified: commonsense explanations, psychological explanations, and stereotype explanations.

Commonsense Explanations

Commonsense explanations of blindness are part of the folklore of our culture.[1] These explanations rest upon the implicit assump-

---

[1] Commonsense assumptions about the blind have been analyzed in detail in the following sources: Harry Best, *Blindness and the Blind in the United States*, The Macmillan Company, New York, 1934, p. 279; Alan G. Gowman, *The War Blind in American Social Structure*, American Foundation for the Blind, New York, 1957, p. 104; and Hector Chevigny and Sydell Braverman, *The Adjustment of the Blind*, Yale University Press, New Haven, 1950, p. 31.

tion that blind people possess personalities and psychologies that are different from those of ordinary people. It is supposed that the blind dwell in a world that is apart from and beyond the one ordinary men inhabit. This world, which is believed to be less gross and materialistic than our own, is said to be infused with a spirituality that gives its inhabitants a peculiar purity and innocence of mind. Those who live in the world of the blind are believed capable of experiencing unique inner feelings and rising to aesthetic heights that are beyond the abilities of all but the most unusual of sighted men. At the same time, this world is thought to be filled with melancholy; expressions of playfulness and humor are out of keeping. Such gloom is said to be cast upon the blind because of their need to settle some great inner conflict. The blind are assumed to be frustrated, cursing their darkness as they reflect back to the days when they could see. They are thought to be helpless, and their abilities are questioned at every turn. It is believed that there are few things a blind man can do for himself, and his mental void precludes any real intellectual development and performance. Helplessness, dependency, melancholy, docility, gravity of inner thought, aestheticism—these are the things that commonsense views tell us to expect of the blind.

Commonsense views hold that the blind are this way because their handicap makes them so. To be unable to see is to be helpless, to live in perpetual darkness is to be melancholic, blindness is dependence, and so on. There is a kind of simplicity to this explanation that makes it appealing. Moreover, observations of certain blind people in everyday life appear to give it some support. There are blind people who are in fact melancholy, helpless, and dependent; there are those among the blind who are given to gravity of inner thought and preoccupation with the spiritual and the aesthetic; and there are others who seem docile and tractable. Don't these observations provide evidence to confirm the commonsense explanation? I think not.

For one thing, the explanations contain a flaw in logic. It is held that the restrictions imposed upon an individual by blindness are both numerous and specific, yet, on close examination, this assumption proves to be erroneous. The only restrictions that this condition imposes result from the fact that the absence of vision prevents a person from relating directly to his distant physical environment.[2] It therefore follows that people who cannot see will be unable to navigate in unfamiliar environments without mechanical aids or assistance from others. People who are totally blind do not have direct access to the printed word, nor can they directly experience such things as distant scenery, paintings, or objects, such as buildings, that are too large to be apprehended by touch. From these restrictions one can readily deduce why people who are totally blind do not engage in certain types of activities such as reading ink print, flying airplanes, or playing tennis. It is logically impossible, however, to deduce that such things as melancholia, spirituality, aestheticism, or helplessness should follow from the nature of this condition itself.

Second, according to the commonsense view, the restrictions that allegedly inhere in blindness lead us to expect certain uniformities in the behavior and attitudes of all people who are totally blind. While such uniformities are found among some blind people, behavioral and adjustment patterns of other subgroups of the blind disconfirm this prediction. Research studies such as Graham's investigation of blinded veterans,[3] Josephson's study of the unserved blind,[4] and the Josephson-Sussman study of the undetected blind;[5] the accomplishments of many individual blind people; and the clinical experiences of blindness workers together provide ample evidence that behavior, attitudes, and patterns of adaptation among the blind are not invariant but quite diverse.

These same data disconfirm the commonsense view in still another way. The predicted attitudinal and behavioral regularities

[2] From a conversation with Professor Roelf G. Boiten, Laboratorium Voor Werkuigkundige Meet-en, Regeltechniek, Technische, Hogeschool, Delft, The Netherlands.

[3] Milton D. Graham *et al., 851 Blinded Veterans: A Success Story,* American Foundation for the Blind, New York, 1968.

[4] Eric Josephson, *The Social Life of Blind People,* Research Series No. 19, American Foundation for the Blind, New York, 1968.

[5] Eric Josephson and Marvin B. Sussman, "A Pilot Study of Visual Impairment," American Foundation for the Blind, New York, 1965, mimeographed.

among the blind are explained as the effects that complete loss of vision is likely to have on individuals. For most purposes, the blindness population is defined as consisting not only of the totally blind, but also of sighted people who have severe vision impairments. The findings of the Josephson study[6] and my own observations of the clients of blindness agencies both suggest that many of the "blind" who can see acquire the attitudes and behavior patterns that the commonsense view says should be found only in the totally blind. This suggests that the so-called invariant behavior patterns may, in fact, be learned, a notion to which I will return shortly.

Psychological Explanations

Psychological explanations proceed from two basic assumptions, that the attitudes and behavior patterns exhibited by the blind are diverse rather than monolithic, and that this diversity is not idiosyncratic, but patterned in a clear, predictable way. This patterning is the result of two factors, the psychological reactions that all blind people have to becoming blind, and the enduring impact of the condition upon basic components of personality. According to this view, people react to the onset of blindness in much the same way. There is the shock that comes from so enormous a blow to self and personality; there is the grief that results from the loss of basic skills for coping with everyday life; and there is the depression that accompanies the disorganization of total personality.[7] Significant variations in attitudes, emotions, and behavior do not occur among blind people until the stage of adjustment begins. Adjustment, according to this theory, implies that the blind person has faced and fully accepted the fact that he is blind, so that he can set out to learn the skills and attitudes that enable him to compensate for the losses he has suffered. If he adjusts, he can then attain independence and a

[6] Josephson, *op. cit.*, Chap. 6.

[7] See H. Robert Blank, "Psychoanalysis and Blindness," *Psychoanalytic Quarterly*, Vol. 26, No. 1, 1957, pp. 1–24; Thomas J. Carroll, *Blindness: What It Is, What It Does, and How to Live with It*, Little, Brown and Company, Boston, 1961; Louis A. Cholden, *A Psychiatrist Works with Blindness*, American Foundation for the Blind, New York, 1958; Louis A. Cholden, "Some Psychiatric Problems in the Rehabilitation of the Blind," *Bulletin of the Menninger Clinic*, Vol. 18, No. 3, 1954, pp. 107–112.

sense of mastery, in which case the behavior patterns that are allegedly inherent in blindness disappear. If he does not adjust, his initial reactions at the onset of blindness stabilize into hard-core attitudes and patterns of behavior.

There is a great deal to be learned about the behavior of the blind from this explanation. By it we are alerted to the dynamics of reactions to the onset of blindness; we get from it a clear sense of what effective rehabilitation must include; and it helps us to explain not just one but two of the basic adaptive patterns that are found among the blind. No explanation of the behavior of the blind can be complete without taking cognizance of the factors to which we are sensitized by this approach.

At the same time, there are certain problems with it. One is that it is extremely difficult, perhaps impossible, to test. Two examples of this problem will illustrate the point. First, this explanation holds that the reactions of blind people following the onset of blindness must follow a predictable and unvarying sequence. But what of the blind man, and there are some, whose reactions do not follow the prescribed course? Is the theory not disconfirmed by such cases? According to its advocates, it is not. The behavior of such blind men is merely a defensive reaction used to avoid confronting the reality they would rather deny. However, if it is asserted that any behavior is defensive that fails to conform to the pattern prescribed by the theory, then how are we to test the theory? How can we put to empirical test a theory of blindness that explains negative cases by placing the fault with blind men rather than with the explanation? Second, the psychological explanation asserts that the only blind man who can diverge from the course set for him by his reactions to blindness is the one who accepts the fact that he is blind and then sets out to compensate for his losses. The evidence adduced to prove this proposition is that adjusted blind people no longer behave in a docile, tractable, melancholy, helpless fashion. The trouble is that we are given no clues as to how to determine if adjustment has occurred independently of the behavior and attitudes that it allegedly produces. The statement is, therefore, a tautological proposition.

A second problem is that data from empirical research studies of the blind, such as they are, suggest that the psychological explanation of the attitudes and behavior of the blind may be overgeneralized. This point can be illustrated by a single example. The psychological explanation implies that the blind man who fails to adjust will continue displaying the attitudes and behavior patterns that were laid down during his initial reactions to blindness. Josephson, in his study of the blind of four states, obtained some data relevant to this proposition. Substantial numbers of people in his sample rejected the idea that they were blind even though their vision loss was severe enough to place them well within the bounds of the currently accepted administrative definition of blindness.[8] According to the psychological explanation, such persons could not have adjusted to their disability, since adjustment requires that they first accept the fact of their blindness. Yet Josephson found that many of these persons were quite independent and able to engage in many of the ordinary activities of daily living. Moreover, he found little evidence of the tension and depression that the psychological explanation of blindness would lead us to expect.[9]

A final criticism of the psychological explanation of blindness is that it attempts to explain the behavior of a blind man solely in terms of the condition's effects upon basic intrapsychic processes. Nowhere is this more apparent than in its application in practice settings. In most of them, the *individual* is the basic unit of rehabilitation, and his attitudes and behavior are the objects of change. I do not wish to imply that this focus on the individual is inappropriate; it is, however, incomplete. It ignores an important fact about the problems of blindness, namely, that they are as much a product of social definition and societal reactions as they are of intrapsychic forces. However erroneous existing stereotypes about blindness may be, they are nevertheless real. No blind man can ignore them, and for most they are central contingencies of his life.[10] To suppose, therefore, that solutions to the problems of blindness can be achieved simply by changing the blind man is to ignore a large part of his problems.

[8] Josephson, *op. cit.*, p. 18.
[9] *Ibid.*, pp. 71–74.
[10] Gowman, *op. cit.*, pp. 5–9.

Stereotype Explanations

A third explanation for the behavior of blind men attempts to deal directly with this aspect; it is called the stereotype theory of blindness.[11] The basic aim of this explanation is to show how misguided commonsense assumptions that laymen make about the blind affect the blind. As we have already suggested in our discussion of commonsense explanations of blindness, many laymen acquire erroneous conceptions about the blind as a by-product of their general socialization. While these beliefs are incorrect, they are also quite real. Sighted people rely upon them whenever they have dealings with the blind; they are expressed in the form of expectations by the sighted for the behavior of the blind. Because of them, true communications are impossible. Even worse, these misconceptions may in time become real patterns of behavior. When, for example, sighted people continually insist that a blind man is helpless because he is blind, their subsequent treatment of him may preclude his ever exercising the kinds of skills that would enable him to be independent. It is in this sense that stereotypic beliefs are self-actualized.

There is much to commend this theory as an explanation for the behavior of the blind. For one thing, it is intensively relevant. It takes as its starting point a core contingency of life for virtually all blind people, that the routine interactions of everyday life are infused with ambiguities, misunderstandings, misperceptions, and frustrations. The stereotype explanation correctly sensitizes us to the unwitting, yet crucial, role that the sighted play in this unhappy state of affairs. Furthermore, it helps to explain one of the main paradoxes about blind people, namely, that the behavior of at least some subgroups of the blind conforms to the stereotypes in spite of the fact that there is nothing about the condition of blindness that makes such behavior necessary.

Though basically sound, there is one difficulty with this theory; it

[11] *Ibid.*; Chevigny and Braverman, *op. cit.*; Joseph S. Himes, "Some Concepts of Blindness in American Culture," *Social Casework*, Vol. 31, No. 10, 1950, pp. 410–416; and Thomas D. Cutsforth, *The Blind in School and Society: A Psychological Study*, American Foundation for the Blind, New York, 1951.

places too strong an emphasis on *beliefs,* while ignoring other factors involved in the reactions sighted people have to the blind. Thus,
the theory asserts that it is the sighted person's beliefs that cause his
reactions to a blind man. In order to explain these intense and far-
reaching reactions, the advocates of this theory have had to postu-
late a highly elaborated, rigid, widely shared stereotype of the blind.
While the empirical evidence on this point does suggest that many
laymen accept as true one or even a few erroneous beliefs about
the blind, it does not support the view that large numbers of laymen
share the elaborate, complicated stereotype that advocates of this
explanation have asserted they do.[12] Two interpretations have been
made of the findings of these studies. The first is that sighted persons' effects upon the blind have simply been exaggerated and that
the core of a blind person's problems is not found in others' actions
and reactions toward him. This interpretation is, I believe, contra-
dicted by the experience of too many blind people.[13] The second, and
more likely, interpretation is that a sighted person's impact upon a
blind man is mediated by more than just his beliefs. Other factors,
having to do with the mechanics of relations between the blind and
the sighted, are also involved, factors with which I deal more fully
in Chapter 2.

The reader should not infer that, because there are limitations to
the psychological and stereotypic explanations of blindness, such
explanations have no utility. On the contrary, I have drawn heavily
on the ideas contained in them.

SOURCES OF DATA IN THIS STUDY

The most difficult problem of this research has been to obtain valid, reliable, and complete data on blind people and blindness agencies. Whenever possible, I have used the findings of past research
studies on blindness and work for the blind. In addition, when they

[12] Irving F. Lukoff and Martin Whiteman, "Attitudes and Blindness:
Components, Correlates and Effects," Washington, D.C., 1963, mimeographed; and Victor Paske and Walter Weiss, "Fitidsun Der Sogelsen,"
Copenhagen, 1965, mimeographed.
[13] Gowman, *op. cit.,* pp. 5–9.

contained usable data, I have analyzed the records and reports of many public and private organizations for the blind. Unfortunately, much of the information in these reports cannot be used for research purposes. Proper precautions were seldom taken to ensure an acceptable degree of accuracy; in many instances, the raw data used to compile the figures contained in the reports are obviously invalid; and the understandable desire of the authors to show progress from one year to the next introduces a serious bias. Consequently, the data in these reports seldom reflect accurately what is in fact occurring in an organization. When I have been able to trace the process by which the data of such reports came into being, so that I could estimate the degree and sources of error they contain, I have used the data for this study.

Next, I conducted nearly one hundred interviews with professional workers in the field of work for the blind, including national leaders in this field; state commissioners for the blind; representatives of all major public and private organizations for the blind; experts in specialized areas such as braille, mobility, social and personal services, employment, and rehabilitation; trustees and members of boards of directors of private organizations for the blind; and numerous rank-and-file workers who implement service programs. The persons I interviewed were carefully selected in order to be certain that all major points of view, issues, and activities in this field were represented. From these interviews I obtained two types of data. The first type relates to the assumptions, ideologies, and theories that act as guidelines for practice in this field. As a result of these interviews, I felt I had uncovered the full range of beliefs that workers hold about such basic questions as why the condition of blindness is a problem at all; how people are supposed to react to the onset of this condition; how they are supposed to feel and behave as blind people; the changes in behavior and attitude they are supposed to undergo as a result of rehabilitation; and what kinds of attitudes and behavior patterns they are expected to display after they have been rehabilitated. The second type of data consists of explanations of the character and inner workings of the field of work for the blind as seen by knowledgeable insiders.

In addition, I spoke with perhaps a hundred blind people to determine their beliefs concerning some matters about which I had questioned workers for the blind. These interviews also produced a wide
variety of other data about the kinds of problems that most concern
them as blind people; how they, as blind people, understand their
problems; their feelings about the organizations and persons who
are trying to help them; and their preferences and desires in life.
These interviews also provided me with detailed accounts of the
experiences some of them had had from the time that they became
blind until the time I had been introduced to them.

The blind people I interviewed came from all kinds of circumstances and situations. Many of them had been clients of agencies
for the blind for many years; some had just come to blindness agencies for help when I first saw them; others had studiously avoided
any contact ever with organizations in the blindness system; and
still others had completely severed the relationships they had once
had with such agencies. My sample included blind people who were
employed competitively, some who were employed in sheltered workshops for the blind, and some who were beggars on the street. It included blind people who were advocates, and often architects, of
the present blindness system and those who were its most bitter
adversaries. Because of the almost total absence of data about both
the blindness and the client populations, I can make no claims about
the representativeness of this sample to the total blindness population, or to that segment of it that includes only clients of organizations. As an observer of this field for nearly three years, however, I
feel reasonably certain that through this sample I have encountered
most of the situations, experiences, and sentiments of blind people
who are clients or former clients of agencies for the blind.

Finally, a great deal of my time in this project was spent visiting
and observing the activities of agencies and programs for the blind.
For nearly two years, my offices were located in one such agency.
This gave me an opportunity to learn a great deal about the assump-
tive world of workers and clients, and to gain an unusually complete view into this agency's internal workings. My observations were
not, however, limited to just one agency. I also spent much time

visiting and observing a representative sample of other organizations, programs, and agencies in the blindness system.

It would be careless to claim that these data are entire and complete for blind people and work for the blind. The truth of this matter cannot be determined until more information has been collected about all aspects of blindness and the blindness field. There are, however, two facts that should be taken into account in evaluating the data of this report. The first is that several segments of my study have been independently replicated by others, and the results of these studies provide substantial confirmation of many of my findings.[14] The second is that I have continuously checked my impressions and conclusions by questioning and requestioning the blindness workers and blind people I found to be most knowledgeable about this field. Their comments have reassured me that my findings have very substantial basis in fact.

One final note of explanation. In any discussion of blindness, it is essential to draw a distinction between those who are born blind and those whose blindness is acquired. The former are usually termed "the congenitally blind" and the latter "the adventitiously blinded," or simply "the blinded." While there are no exact figures on the number of people in each of these subgroups of the blindness population, it is clear that no more than a tiny fraction of all blind people are congenitally blind. There is a consensus among blindness workers that the dynamics of personality development and of social functioning of a congenitally blind person are substantially different from those of someone who is adventitiously blinded.[15] Because of these differences, I have restricted my analysis to the adventitiously blinded. That is not, of course, to imply in any way that the problems of the congenitally blind are less significant or less interesting than those of the blinded.[16] It is simply a matter of the impossibility of focusing on both groups simultaneously.

[14] "An Analysis of Blindness and Services to the Blind in the United States," Organization for Social and Technical Innovation, Boston, 1967, mimeographed.

[15] Carroll, *op. cit.*, pp. 277–281.

[16] Robert A. Scott, "The Socialization of the Blind Child," in David A. Goslin, ed., *The Handbook of Socialization Theory and Research*, Rand McNally & Company, Chicago, 1969.

CHAPTER 1

The Socialization of the Blind

*T*HE disability of blindness is a learned social role. The various attitudes and patterns of behavior that characterize people who are blind are not inherent in their condition but, rather, are acquired through ordinary processes of social learning. Thus, there is nothing inherent in the condition of blindness that requires a person to be docile, dependent, melancholy, or helpless; nor is there anything about it that should lead him to become independent or assertive. Blind men are made, and by the same processes of socialization that have made us all. The purpose of this book is to demonstrate this thesis.

Basic to my analysis is the idea of the self-concept.[1] By "self-concept" I mean an individual's perception of himself. A man's self-concept consists of the attitudes, feelings, and beliefs he has about the kind of a person he is, his strengths and weaknesses, his

[1] George H. Mead, *Mind, Self and Society*, ed. by Charles W. Morris, University of Chicago Press, Chicago, 1940.

14

potentials and limitations, his characteristic qualities, and so forth. These things are expressed both in his actions and in his responses to the questions, "Who am I?" and "What kind of a person am I?" A man's self-concept, or his personal identity if you prefer, is at the heart of his experience as a socialized human being. His subjective experience of the world is colored by it; his actions and reactions to others are filtered through it; and his behavior in most situations is guided by it. To know the kind of an image that a man has of himself is, therefore, to understand a great deal about him.

A self-concept is not given to a man when he is born; rather, it is something he acquires as he is socialized. Inherent in self-concept is the ability to take self as an object of its own perception; to do this, in turn, a person must learn to view himself from the point of view of other people. The child who plays at the role of parent and thereby learns to see and respond to himself as his parents do, and the adult who takes the perspective of the group or the community at large in order to imagine how "they" are likely to react to his anticipated behavior, are both involved in getting outside themselves and looking back on their own behavior. Self-image cannot develop without taking the role of another vis-à-vis oneself. Because of this, the substance of a man's self-image largely consists of his perceptions of the evaluations that others make of him, and particularly those others whose opinions he values most highly.

These evaluations that are made of us by others, and that we internalize as a part of our self-concept, can be thought of as expressions of expectations of behavior, as indications of how we are doing relative to how others expect us to do. These expectations tend to be uniform. Most adults, for example, are in general agreement about how children ought to behave, and most of them also hold certain relatively uniform expectations of the behavior of other specific categories of people, such as men, women, old people, young people, whites, blacks, married people, single people, doctors, or street cleaners. There is, then, a certain consensus about how individuals who fall into different categories ought to behave. Indeed, it is as though a putative social identity exists for the various categories of people in our culture. Whenever we recognize an individual as belonging to a particular category, we impute to him the social identity reserved for persons in it, and we evaluate him in terms of whether or not his behavior conforms to this putative social identity. To the extent that an individual correctly perceives our evaluations of him and internalizes them as part of his self-concept, this putative social identity becomes a personal identity in fact. This process of role learning is termed "socialization."

What has this to do with the ways blind people experience their blindness? At the core of any blind man's experience of blindness are the attitudes, beliefs, and feelings he has about the kind of person he is, what he is capable of doing, how he is supposed to feel, how he is different from others, how he is like others, and so forth. These things are the substance of his self-concept. They are acquired through ordinary processes of socialization, in which he is rewarded for behaving in ways that conform to the putative social identity reserved for the blind and sanctioned for behaving in ways that do not conform. These role-learning processes occur in three principal contexts.[2] The first is in early childhood. A part of the socialization experience in any society involves learning attitudes, beliefs, and values about stigmatized people such as the blind. These beliefs concern the effects that the condition is alleged to have on personality, and how a person who becomes blind is changed because of it. It is by reference to these beliefs that a putative social identity for the blind is constructed. When the blindness belongs to ourselves, these beliefs we have acquired about blindness become internal guidelines for our own behavior. In this sense, we have all in a general way learned the role of blind man; however, for most of us, it is a role we will never have to play.

The second context in which people who cannot see learn the social role of blind person is in face-to-face interactions with people who can see. In such encounters, the beliefs and assumptions about blindness that have been learned through early socialization become the expectations that others have for the blind person's behavior. To the extent that a blind man accepts the imputations made to him

---

[2] Orville G. Brim, Jr., and Stanton Wheeler, *Socialization after Childhood*, John Wiley & Sons, Inc., New York, 1967.

by people who see, his conception of self as helpless, docile, dependent, or incapacitated is reinforced. Even if he rejects these assertions as false, however, they may nevertheless become a reality. The assumption, for example, that blindness is incapacitating may lead those who hold it to deny the blind person any opportunity to exercise the skills by which he might attain independence or mastery.[3] Furthermore, the conduct of ordinary personal relationships depends very heavily on sight. In its absence, many of the norms of ordinary interaction can no longer be applied; as a result, relationships between the sighted and the blind are often strained and infused with ambiguity. From the uncertain responses of sighted people to them, blind people draw inferences (often erroneous ones) about the probable beliefs and assumptions that must underlie such reactions. To the extent that these beliefs and assumptions are internalized, they become part of the blind man's self-concept. At the very least, these idiosyncratic reactions serve to emphasize to the blind person how different he is from others.

The third context in which blind people learn the behavior patterns and attitudes associated with their disability is in the organizations that have been established for the purpose of helping blind people. In highly industrialized societies such as our own, the responsibility for the management, control, and rehabilitation of blind people is vested primarily in specialized organizations, most of which are large, complex, bureaucratic structures. It is difficult to exaggerate the important role such organizations play in the socialization of the blind. For one thing, blindness organizations are legion. In this study, I was able to identify over 800 separate agencies, organizations, and facilities for the blind in the United States. There are no major cities in this country that do not have several blindness agencies; virtually every medium-sized urban area has its own privately supported agency for the blind; and there are very few small communities in which at least some services are not available to blind citizens. When it is realized that there are probably no more than a million blind people in this country, it becomes apparent how sig-

[3] Hector Chevigny and Sydell Braverman, *The Adjustment of the Blind*, Yale University Press, New Haven, 1950.

nificant a factor such organizations can become in the lives of people
who are blind.

Through this complicated network of organizations, agencies, and
programs for the blind, the phenomenon of blindness in our society
has literally been transformed. By virtue of the fact that they
exist, blindness organizations become crucial to many blind people.[4] For some, these organizations represent opportunity structures within which careers can develop and grow; for others, they
are places to go for help or recreation; for still others, they are
places—often the only ones—in which remunerative employment
can be secured; and, for some, they are places to be avoided at all
costs. Thus, whether blind people willingly go to blindness agencies
for assistance or are forced to go there because no other alternatives
exist, whether the services they receive are welcomed and helpful
or resisted and obsolete, the blindness network is a factor with
which many blind people must contend. For this reason, a complete
understanding of the behavior of the blind is not possible without
taking into account the network of blindness organizations in which
they are immersed.

Concomitant with the growth of organizations for the blind, a profession related to blindness has developed. It is called "work for the
blind," and its practitioners are known as "workers for the blind" or
simply "blindness workers." The legitimacy of this profession is in
large part based upon its practitioners' claims to specialized knowledge and expertise concerning problems of blindness. Through the
years, this knowledge and expertise have become increasingly formalized, so that in blindness organizations today there are a number
of more or less distinct approaches to blindness. These approaches
are based on beliefs and assumptions concerning the fundamental
problems experienced by people who are blind, the necessary and appropriate solutions to these problems, and the reactions of people
when they first become blind and during each successive stage of
their rehabilitation. These beliefs and assumptions serve to guide
practitioners in dealing with clients in the clinical setting of the

[4] Howard S. Becker, *Outsiders: Studies in the Sociology of Deviance*, The
Free Press of Glencoe, New York, 1963, p. 9.

blindness agency. The approaches are expressed as the blindness workers' expectations of the attitudes and behavior of those they are trying to help. For blindness workers, one key indicator of the success of a rehabilitation endeavor is the degree to which the client has come to understand himself and his problems from the workers' perspective. While he learns to understand himself from this perspective the blind person is also acquiring blindness-related attitudes and behavior patterns that "go along with" his rehabilitators' approach. Thus it is that, through the same mechanisms that operate in personal relationships, many of the attitudes, behavior patterns, and feelings at the core of a blind person's self-concept are learned from blindness workers in the context of agencies for the blind. The distinctive feature of much of this role learning is that it is overt and goal-directed; its explicit aim is to instill in blind people certain model behavior patterns and attitudes.

CHAPTER 2

The Socialization of the Blind

in Personal Interaction

ONE OF the ways in which a person who has difficulty seeing learns how to be a blind man is by interacting with those who see. When normals come face-to-face with someone who cannot see, their preconceptions about, and reactions to, blindness are expressed as expectations of how the blind man ought to behave. The blind man is poignantly reminded of the social identity imputed to him by others. All blind men respond to this identity in some way, even if only to dispute it; for those who internalize it, this putative social identity becomes a personal identity in fact.

There are two principal mechanisms of personal encounters through which the blind are socialized. The first relates to preconceptions about blindness that people who can see bring to encounters with blind men, the second to the reactions of the sighted during the encounter. Normal people will react to a blind man as a blind man only if they perceive him as such. The interpersonal context of the socialization of the blind applies, therefore, only to those blind people whose blindness is readily apparent to others. Most laymen know little or nothing about the technical definitions of blindness that professionals use, and even those who do cannot make the fine discriminations that are required in order to determine where someone whose vision is severely impaired falls relative to the line set by the definition. The socialization processes described in this chapter apply, therefore, to people who are totally or virtually blind, and whose impairment is readily identifiable as such.

PRECONCEPTIONS ABOUT BLINDNESS

The preconceptions that the sighted bring to situations of interaction with the blind are of two sorts. On the one hand, there are stereotypic beliefs about blindness and the blind that they have acquired through the ordinary processes of socialization in our culture; and, on the other, there is the fact that blindness is a stigmatizing condition. Each factor makes its special contribution to the social identity that is reserved for blind men. As I suggested in the introduction, the notions of a blindness stereotype and of blindness as stigma have already received a good deal of attention in the literature.[1] Little would be gained, therefore, by a simple reiteration of these ideas. My purpose here is to place the stereotype and stigma notions into the perspective of this book by explaining the contributions each makes to the self-concept that a blind man acquires.

Stereotypic Beliefs about Blindness

In my introduction I described a number of the general beliefs that laymen have about the blind. These beliefs involve notions of helplessness, docility, dependency, melancholia, aestheticism, and serious-mindedness. While few laymen accept all these beliefs, most

[1] See Harry Best, *Blindness and the Blind in the United States*, Macmillan Company, New York, 1934, p. 279; Hector Chevigny and Sydell Braverman, *The Adjustment of the Blind*, Yale University Press, New Haven, 1950, p. 26; and Alan G. Gowman, *The War Blind in American Social Structure*, American Foundation for the Blind, New York, 1957, p. 104.

of them do adhere to at least a few of them. These misconceptions are brought by them to situations of interaction with the blind and are expressed as expectations of the behavior and attitudes of the blind person. Because of them, deep and stubborn "grooves and channels" are created into which all the blind man's actions and feelings are pressed. Their existence makes it extremely difficult for meaningful communication and unstrained relationships to occur between the seeing and the blind.

The effects such beliefs have upon blind people when they interact with sighted people have been succinctly described by Gowman:

An individual taking up the role of blind man is conceptually relocated along the margins of the dominant social structure and a peripheral social role is assigned to him. His rights and obligations are redefined in a manner which is believed to mesh with the character of the disability. The newly blinded person is reevaluated in all his aspects, and the evaluative scale shifts from the measurement of specific individual qualities or capabilities to the assessment of the global condition of blindness. What distinguishes the blind role from other types of roles is its all pervasive character. Blindness is not an attribute to be put on or cast off as the situation demands, but a constant characteristic which affects the quality of each of the individual's relationships in occupational, recreational, and other contexts. When evaluation is thus expanded to cover an individual's entire personality structure, a stereotype is operative. The blind may be assigned a social role which so transforms them that they emerge as a labeled segment of society. Social interaction becomes stunted and artificial under the impress of the stereotype.[2]

It is impossible for blind men to ignore these beliefs; they have no choice but to respond to them. These responses vary, but in a highly patterned way. Some blind people come to concur in the verdict that has been reached by those who see. They adopt as a part of their self-concept the qualities of character, the feelings, and the behavior patterns that others insist they must have. Docility, helplessness, melancholia, dependency, pathos, gratitude, a concern for the spiritual and the aesthetic, all become a genuine part of the blind man's personal identity. Such blind men might be termed "true believers";

[2] Gowman, *op. cit.*, p. 46.

they have become what others with whom they interact assume they must become because they are blind.

Not all blind people are true believers; there are many who explicitly, indeed insistently, reject the imputations made of them by others. They thereby manage to insulate a part of the self-concept from the assaults made on it by normals. The personal identity of such a person is not that of a blind man, but of a basically normal person who cannot see. For the blind man who responds in this way, there remains the problem that most people who see do not share the view he has reached about himself. Some blind men respond simply by complying with the expectations of the sighted, in a conscious and deliberate way. They adopt an external facade that is consistent with the normals' assumptions about them, but they are aware that it is a facade, and they are ready to drop it whenever occasions permit them to do so. Ordinarily, the reason for acquiescence is expedience; in fact, every blind man, whether he accepts or rejects the social identity imputed to him, will be found to acquiesce at least some of the time. For example, several blind people have told me that when they use public transportation, fellow passengers will occasionally put money into their hands. When this occurs, a blind man cannot very well give a public lecture on the truth about blindness; in fact, to do anything but acquiesce and accept the gift will leave him open to charges of ingratitude and bitterness. There are other blind people who use the acquiescent facade not for expedience but as a weapon. Those who beg, for example, deliberately cultivate it in order to encourage people to give them money. The beggar strikes up an unstated pact with the world: he agrees to behave exactly as others insist that he must, and in exchange he makes the normal person pay with money. How dear this price is, of course, depends upon the beggar's ability to exploit the emotions that lead his victims to expect him to acquiesce in the first place.

Another way that blind men cope with discrepancies between putative and personal identity is to resist and negate the imputations of others at every turn. By so doing, personal integrity is preserved, but the cost is very high. It requires an enormous commitment and expenditure of energy to resist these forces, and the blind man who does so inevitably alienates himself from other people. Even those who follow this road successfully are left with a certain bitterness and frustration that is the inevitable residue of any attempt to break the stubborn molds into which the blind man's every action is pressed.

Clearly, then, these stereotypic beliefs about the blind have profound consequences for the self-concept of every blind man. He may internalize them as a part of his self-image, or he may reject them as completely false and misleading, but he cannot ignore them. The fact that he cannot is one of the several reasons why homogeneity develops in this otherwise heterogenous group of individuals.

Blindness as Stigma

Blindness is a stigma, carrying with it a series of moral imputations about character and personality. The stereotypical beliefs I have discussed lead normal people to feel that the blind are different; the fact that blindness is a stigma leads them to regard blind men as their physical, psychological, moral, and emotional inferiors. Blindness is therefore a trait that discredits a man by spoiling both his identity and his respectability.

When a person with a stigma encounters a normal person, barriers are created between them.[3] These barriers, though symbolic, are often impenetrable. They produce a kind of "moving away," much like the action of two magnetized particles of metal whose similar poles have been matched. These avoidance reactions are often induced by a fear that direct contact with a blind person may be contaminating, or that the stigmatized person will somehow inflict physical or psychic damage. Such reactions and fears are completely emotional and irrational in character.

The effects of these reactions on a blind man are profound. Even though he thinks of himself as a normal person, he recognizes that most others do not really accept him, nor are they willing or ready

[3] Fred Davis, "Deviance Disavowal: The Management of Strained Interaction by the Visibly Handicapped," in Howard S. Becker, ed., *The Other Side*, The Free Press of Glencoe, New York, 1964, pp. 119–138, and Robert Kleck, Ono Hiroshi, and Albert H. Hastorf, "The Effects of Physical Deviance upon Face-to-Face Interaction," *Human Relations*, Vol. 19, No. 4, 1966, pp. 425–436.

to deal with him on an equal footing. Moreover, as Goffman has observed, "the standards he has incorporated from the wider society equip him to be intimately alive to what others see as his failure, inevitably causing him, if only for moments, to agree that he does indeed fall short of what he really ought to be."[4] As a result, he may feel shame because he knows he possesses a defiling attribute. It is when the blind person finds himself in the company of the sighted that these self-derogating feelings are aroused. "The central feature of the stigmatized individual's situation in life," writes Goffman, "is a question of what is often, if vaguely, called 'acceptance.' Those who have dealings with him fail to accord him the respect and regard which the uncontaminated aspects of his social identity have led them to anticipate extending and have led him to anticipate receiving; he echoes this denial by finding that some of his own attributes warrant it."[5]

The stigma of blindness makes problematic the integrity of the blind man as an acceptable human being. Because those who see impute inferiority, the blind man cannot ignore this and is forced to defend himself. If, as sometimes occurs, the blind man shares the values of the sighted, the process becomes even more insidious; for when this is the case, a man's personal identity is open to attack from within as well as from without.

THE SITUATION OF INTERACTION

Preconceptions about blindness are not the only elements of personal encounters that determine a blind man's socialization experiences; certain features of the actual encounter play an important role as well. First of all, the norms governing ordinary personal interaction cannot, as a rule, be applied when one of the actors is unable to see. Furthermore, blind people, because they cannot see, must rely for assistance upon the seeing with whom they interact. As a result, many of the interactions that involve the sighted and blind men become relationships of social dependency. Each of these factors

[4] Erving Goffman, *Stigma: Notes on the Management of Spoiled Identity*, Prentice-Hall, Inc., Englewood Cliffs, N.J., 1963, p. 7.
[5] *Ibid.*, pp. 8–9.

is intimately related to the kind of self-concept the blind man develops, and, because of them, this group of people is made even more homogeneous.

Blindness and the Conduct of Personal Relationships

Vision plays an extremely important role in the face-to-face encounters of everyday life. The initial impressions we have of people are acquired largely through vision, and the success of our subsequent relationships with them depends to a considerable extent on our ability to see. It is when one of the actors is blind that we recognize how central a part vision plays in our relationships with other people.

ESTABLISHING AN IDENTITY. One of the things we do upon meeting someone for the first time is to impute to him a familiar social identity. We label him elderly, handsome, debonair, cultured, timid, or whatever. From the identity we have imputed to him, we anticipate what his tastes and interests will be, the kinds of attitudes he will have, and how he is likely to behave. We search for clues to help us to classify the person as a type of individual, and we then apply norms of conduct associated with "his type" in order to guide us in our subsequent interaction with him. Unless we can do this quickly and accurately, we are at a loss as to how to proceed, and experience the situation as embarrassing and stressful.

What people wear, how they look, the way they stand, and the gestures they use are important clues in helping us to reach some decision about the type of person we have encountered. Indeed, most of the initial impressions we form of persons are based on clues that must be seen to be detected. For this reason, initial encounters between the seeing and the blind are set awry; since one actor is blind, each is deprived of significant information about the other. The blind person will be at a loss to know precisely with whom he is dealing, and what kind of behavior to expect from him. He will be slow to piece together the information he needs correctly to infer the person's social identity. This produces an ambiguity and uneasiness that can become so intense that the relationship never develops.

The inability to gather accurate information on which to form impressions is not a problem only for the blind person; it leads to uneasiness on the part of the sighted individual as well. He is uncertain that the image he tries to project will be received, or, if received, accurately interpreted. He will realize immediately that his general appearance is no longer useful for conveying information about himself. His uneasiness intensifies if he does not know which nonvisual clues the blind man is using to "size him up." Is it the tone of voice or the content of words? Does his tone of voice convey something about himself that he is unaware of or wishes to conceal? He does not know how to convey to the blind man an impression equivalent to the one conveyed through sight. When visual clues to a person's social identity are missing, a difficult and awkward situation is created for both the blind man, who does not develop a complete impression, and the sighted man, who is unsure of the impression he has made.

Conversely, there is the process of social identification of the blind person by the sighted individual. In addition to the stigmatizing quality of blindness, blind people may be insensitive to the role of visual factors in projecting accurate impressions, or they may not know how to create the kind of impression they want to. In this regard, the blind person is dependent upon others. They select his clothes and advise him on his posture. To some extent, then, his appearance is dependent on the tastes of his helpers. Clearly, ambiguities and uncertainties surround the identity of the blind man as well as that of those who see.

NORMS GOVERNING PERSONAL INTERACTION. These ambiguities and uncertainties will sometimes cause the encounter to terminate prematurely. If not, initial uncertainties are carried into the next stage of the relationship, for it is on the basis of initial impressions that we know what to expect of others, and how we should behave toward them. The rules that are applied to an individual on the basis of our identification of him, and the rules that he in turn applies to us, lend structure and substance to the relationship. Since a person's blindness tends to overwhelm those with whom he interacts, it is the blindness more than anything else that identifies him. Blindness is a comparatively rare event in any population, so that only a few sighted individuals ever interact with a blind man in any sustained way. What most of us know about blindness comes from the mass media, religious and other writings, common sense, hearsay, or from occasional contacts with a salesman of products made by the blind, or the solicitor from the local blindness agency. When we encounter a blind man, the rules we apply to him are extremely vague; they tell us what to expect in only the most tentative way. Our lack of direct experience makes the situation more uncertain. This normative ambiguity, indeed normlessness, applies as much to the blind person's understanding of the sighted individual's behavior as it applies to the sighted individual's understanding of how to behave with a blind person. In this sense, the difficulty lies with the relationship and not with the individual partners to it.

One facet of this problem deserves special emphasis. Easy social interaction is contingent upon the possession of certain skills and information that can be used as a conversation goes along. I have in mind here the most elementary kinds of things. For example, when a person meets me in my office, I may invite him to take a seat. He may wish to have a cup of coffee and a cigarette. Perhaps we will share lunch together either in my office or in a restaurant. He may wish to use the telephone while we visit. I may want to show him written materials, or he may have to excuse himself to use the bathroom. Easy, uninterrupted communication hinges on the ability of both of us to carry out the activities necessary to the encounter with ease and independence. Let us go back over the encounter as I have described it and assume that this person is blind. When he enters my office, I find I cannot simply invite him to take a seat but must conduct him to it. As I approach him, I realize that I do not know how to direct him easily, and he does not know if I can do so either. Consequently, we share an awkward moment as I try to lead him to a chair and back him into it. He in turn tries to accept my assistance gracefully while trying not to be impaled by the arms of the chair. After he is seated, I offer him coffee. When it arrives, I realize that he may want cream and sugar. It is unclear if he can manage this himself. If he cannot, and he asks me to do it for him, I may place the coffee in front of him only to find that he knocks it over when reaching for it. When lighting a cigarette, he may put a match to it yet fail to ignite it. If he continues to puff away, do I tell him or let him discover it for himself? Suppose that he flicks ashes on himself; do I point this out to him and therefore bring his disability into the conversation or do I let it pass unnoticed? When he asks to use the bathroom, what do I do? How do I direct him to a toilet or urinal or get him to the washstand? We enter a restaurant for lunch, and I realize that he cannot read the menu. How do I help him to get seated at the table? He orders meat and the question arises as to whether or not he is able to cut it. And what about things on the table of which he is unaware, such as butter and rolls? How do I help him to get these things? From its inception to its conclusion, the interaction is filled with uncertainty, awkwardness, and ambiguity, making such meetings frustrating, embarrassing, and tense.[6]

Sighted people may try to avoid situations in which such encounters are likely to occur, but there will always be occasions when this is impossible. No one can very well walk away from a blind man who is obviously lost in a crowded street; he cannot ignore the blind man who is about to walk into the side of a building or into an open ditch; he cannot shun the blind person during intimate social gatherings. When normals and blind men are coerced into relationships with one another, most normals fall back on common sense. The trouble with commonsense ideas about the blind is that they are often ridiculous. One man, for example, asked a student in a school for the blind how he knew when he was awake. Another once reprimanded a blind man who had walked into the side of a building for failing to "look out" where he was going. Still another expressed amazement that all a blind man had to do in order to get around a city was to tell his seeing-eye dog the address he wanted and hang on. A blind person can expect anything to happen when he meets a sighted person for the first time. It is almost impossible for him to

[6] Alan G. Gowman, "Blindness and the Role of the Companion," *Social Problems*, Vol. 4, No. 1, 1956, pp. 68–75.

know how the sighted person will react to him. This fact makes for frustrating uncertainties on the part of both parties to the encounter. It has an added consequence for the blind person. He interprets sighted peoples' responses to him as additional evidence that, in their world, the blind are different and lesser people. Why else would sighted people be so insensitive to the blind man's problems, or so anxious to terminate encounters with him? This interpretation by the blind only serves to reinforce the sense of their differentness that is already implied in the preconceptions about blindness.

The effects of uncertainty and ambiguity do not end when the encounter does. The memory of them lingers, giving rise to the impulse to avoid another such experience. Normative ambiguity is, therefore, one of the several reasons many sighted people impulsively act to avoid contact with blind people. It is to be noted in passing that such impulses are accompanied by considerable guilt.

COMMUNICATION PROBLEMS.   Vision plays an enormously important role in personal communication. When we speak to someone, it is customary for us to maintain eye contact. This is learned from the earliest age, so that by about the time a child begins school, this very important lesson has been learned. To turn away or focus on a distant object when addressing another person can be attributed to rudeness, shyness, or guilt. Frequently, the lack of visual contact is one of the factors responsible for the statement, "We simply could not communicate." Eye contact signifies honesty, directness, attentiveness, respect, and a variety of other virtues that are the important ingredients of successful human communication.

The important role of vision in personal interaction has many implications for the blind. The blind person is often able to follow a conversation more closely by turning his ear to the speaker. He may therefore develop the disconcerting habit of turning his head slightly away from the speaker's face. The speaker reacts as he would to a sighted individual turning away—he is not sure the listener is attentive.

But the problem is more complicated than this. In addition to the fact that the blind person may incline his head this way or that to maximize sound, the appearance of his eyes may be disconcerting. When blindness is due to accident, the face and eyes may be disfigured. Sometimes the eyes bulge or are set at peculiar angles; in other cases, they may be opaque or gray. When a person is losing vision, he may also lose the ability to control the eye muscles, so that the eyes constantly flutter and roll about in their sockets. These deformities present major difficulties in communication, because eye contact may be not only disturbing but repulsive to the observer.

Blindness prevents the blind person from getting visual feedback for his own body gestures. This may result in the inadvertent development of gestures and bodily movements that are disruptive of communication. A person who cannot observe his own expressions or others' reactions to them becomes insensitive to the importance of facial and bodily gestures in communication. The blind man often appears to be smiling the smile of a simpleton, or gesturing in a way that makes him appear retarded or mentally deranged. Once again, his unusual facial and body gestures are interpreted as they would be if he could see. This is especially a problem among the congenitally blind, who, out of a need for stimulation, develop peculiar body movements called "blindisms." They probe at the face, tilt the body and roll it, move up and down and back and forth, and often have ticks and twitches of the face. If the sighted person interprets these gestures as being responsive to what he has said, further misunderstandings in communication arise. Conversely, the gesture as a mechanism of communication by the sighted person is also eliminated, which limits the range of expressions he can use. These problems with communication serve to heighten the already difficult misunderstandings that have been created by normative ambiguity.

These three problems of establishing the desired personal identity in the mind of the other actor, of uncertainty as to how to interact with a blind man, and of miscommunication all work together to produce that peculiar blend of annoyance, frustration, ambiguity, anger, tension, and irritation that describes human interaction that is spoiled. The important point is that the source of this unhappy

outcome is not to be found so much in the erroneous beliefs that
the seeing hold about blindness, although such beliefs clearly are not
entirely innocent; rather, it lies in what might be called "the mechanics" of interpersonal conduct. In this sense, the problem lies
more with the relationship itself than with the erroneous conceptions
held by those who are parties to it.

All of this has two important effects on the blind man's self-
concept. First, he is once again reminded that he is different from
most people and that the satisfying personal relationships that are
commonplace to them are, for the most part, denied to him. Second,
because so many of his relationships with other people are spoiled,
he is denied the kind of honest and direct feedback that is so essential for maintaining clear and realistic conceptions about the kind
of person he is.[7] Often the blind man gets no feedback at all, and
when he does it is usually badly distorted. As a result, the blind man
can easily acquire either an unduly negative or an unreasonably
positive conception of his own abilities.

Even though many of the problems that characterize encounters
between sighted and blind men arise from the mechanics of interpersonal conduct, it does not always follow that blind men explain
these problems to themselves in this way. On the contrary, many
of them apparently assume that a normal person's behavior is caused
by his beliefs. Thus, when a sighted person behaves assertively
toward a blind man so as to eliminate uncertainty, the blind man
infers that the other's actions are caused by a belief that blindness
makes him helpless. It is for this reason, I think, that blind people
have placed so much stock in the notion of an elaborate, rigid
stereotype of the blind.

Blindness and Social Dependency

Interactions between the blind and the sighted become relationships of social dependency. To explain why this occurs, it is necessary
to digress for a moment in order to clarify some of the factors that

[7] Stephen A. Richardson, "The Effects of Physical Disability on the Socialization of a Child," in David A. Goslin, ed., *Handbook of Socialization Theory
and Research,* Rand McNally & Company, Chicago, 1969.

enter into ordinary personal relationships.[8] A useful starting point is to ask the question, "Why do people enter into associations with one another?" One answer is, because most of the things that men find pleasurable in life can be obtained only through associations with other people. Some of these associations, such as those which occur between close friends, are rewarding in and of themselves. Other associations are extrinsically rewarding. By this I mean that the partners to the interaction derive particular benefits from social relations because those with whom they interact provide them with a service or fulfill a personal need. Extrinsically rewarding relationships are among the most troublesome of all relationships in which blind people engage; for this reason, I will be concerned primarily with them.

A characteristic of most persons is their liking to help others and do things for them. When we do a favor for someone, he usually feels grateful, and the gratitude he expresses becomes the reward we obtain for having helped him. This is particularly the case if he is vocal in his gratitude, since public expressions of gratitude go a long way toward establishing a good reputation for the person who has rendered the favor. In addition to the fact that we receive gratitude in exchange for favors, we know from experience that rendering a favor will often result in receiving one. When we do someone a favor, he is not only grateful to us; he feels obligated to us. In order to discharge his obligation, he reciprocates by doing something for us. There develops through this circular reciprocity a social bond that is the heart of lasting associations between people. Another reward that is sought in association with others is social approval. The social approval of others, especially of those whose opinions we most value, is of great significance to us. It acts as a curb on our tendency to become too selfish in associations with others. If, in our relations with others, we are too egoistic, we lose social approval. To gain social support requires us to give to others a bit more than we get, or at least not to try to gain more than we give.

---

[8] See Peter M. Blau, *Exchange and Power in Social Life,* John Wiley & Sons, Inc., New York, 1964; and George C. Homans, *Social Behavior,* Harcourt, Brace & World, New York, 1961.

Given the fact, then, that men associate with one another out of a desire to obtain the social rewards of gratitude, reciprocity, and social approval, we may now wonder why people associate differentially with one another. What determines who will associate with whom?

Social attraction is the force that impels men to establish social relations with one another. One person will be attracted to another if he anticipates that associating with him will result in some rewards for him. His desire for social rewards and his perception of the probability of their realization motivate one person to associate with another.

Attraction of one person to another will result in social exchange. This is so because the person who is attracted to another also wants to prove himself attractive to the other, since his ability to associate with him and reap the benefits expected from the association is contingent on the other finding him an attractive associate. Mutual attraction depends upon the anticipation that the association between persons will be mutually rewarding, and social attraction ultimately leads to social exchange. The people involved, however, are not always social equals. There are situations in which A needs what B is able to supply, but A has nothing that B needs. To be sure, the supplier in this exchange may feel rewarded by expressions of gratitude that will most certainly be forthcoming from A; but, if the association is to be durable and long-lasting, it will be necessary for A to provide a compensatory reward in exchange for what B is supplying. What are the alternatives that A might follow? If he is capable of it, he may be able to force B to help him by employing either physical force or social coercion. But this implies that A has a high degree of control over a situation, something he seldom, in fact, has. A second alternative is to seek the rewards he wishes elsewhere, perhaps through someone with whom he can develop an equitable exchange. The final alternative is to forego the satisfaction of the reward. Which alternatives are viable or even possible will depend upon the individuals involved, the intensity of the need, and the structure of the situation. There will be many situations in which none of these alternatives is feasible, and in these cases A has no choice but to exchange the favors given by *B* for compliance with *B's* requests. In this case, the compliance of one person is the reward a supplier receives for the services he renders. Compliance with the demands of others is the substance of power and, for this reason, willingness to comply with the wishes of others is often a very generous reward. It can be seen, incidentally, that exchange processes give rise to differentiation of power among persons, since there will always be some people who are capable of providing services that others need. Power is attained when the supplier makes the satisfaction of those in need contingent on their compliance with his wishes.

In forming extrinsic social relationships, we continually evaluate one another in terms of potential attractiveness. We assess visible and inferred qualities to get some impression about whether or not other persons are potential providers of the services we require. If we decide that the other will be able to meet our needs, sustained social relations become possible. If we decide otherwise, our relationships will either terminate or become casual. Since people seek services from others in exchange for things they want, it follows that people with roughly equivalent, but somewhat different, potentials will be attracted to one another. People will be reluctant to enter into encounters they believe will force them either into too great a degree of compliance (when they are receivers) or (when they are suppliers) into a position in which the compliance of the receiver is not worth the services rendered. For these reasons, "social likes" tend to attract "social likes."

A number of basic problems in personal associations between the blind and the sighted are clarified by viewing them from the perspective of social exchange theory. A person's evaluation of the potential social attractiveness of another will be radically affected if the person evaluated cannot see. Most sighted people will assume that they will have to offer more services to the blind man than the blind man will be able to offer them. Moreover, since blind persons require assistance in getting about in their environment, they will be automatically put into the sighted person's debt. This implies that persons cannot realistically expect to receive payment in kind for favors rendered. That this is recognized in our culture is evident from the fact that most encounters involving the blind and the sighted are defined as charitable. In charitable relationships, the donor person is expected to give generously to the one who is stigmatized, and not to expect to receive anything in return. Actually, this commonly held belief is only partly true, since the charitable person is repaid in part by the fact that his giving is usually public and therefore results in social approval and in part by receiving gratitude. But social approval and gratitude are not in themselves sufficient to sustain relationships. Reciprocity, to be genuine, must involve both socially valued compliance and the capacity to perform socially valued favors.

The blind person is, therefore, by virtue of his dependency, the subordinate in a power relationship. As a rule, none of the alternatives available to subordinates in power relationships are open to him. He cannot forego the service required, since performing important activities of daily life depends on the cooperation of sighted persons. It is unlikely that he will turn elsewhere, partly because he cannot always do that on his own and partly because his situation will be unlikely to change greatly if he does. Finally, he cannot very well rely on force to have favors done for him. He is, therefore, backed into a position of compliance.

Persons who are in positions of power must weigh the cost of granting a service to someone against the potential value of his compliance. Because of his marginal status, a blind man's compliance is only of limited worth to those who seek to gain powerful positions in the mainstream of society. Furthermore, the value of a blind person's compliance may be offset by the investment of time and effort required to render the service. For these reasons, many sighted people avoid encounters with the blind because they anticipate that the compliance of a blind person will be of little value to them. Once again, such avoidance is not achieved without feeling guilt. These guilt feelings become apparent whenever the blind and the sighted are thrust into one another's company.

These factors have several consequences for the blind person's socialization experiences in personal relationships. For one thing, since blindness is a social debit, it follows that blind persons will find it difficult to develop enduring associations with sighted persons who are otherwise their intellectual, psychological, and social equals. The fact that many blind people are not treated as "normal" in this respect is the motive behind a common reaction pattern in the blind. Some blind people disavow their blindness entirely by learning how to perform activities that are normally reserved for people who can see. These include such activities as skiing, golfing, driving auto- mobiles, or doing elaborate repairs on the house. While such activities can be performed by certain blind people, competence in them is attained at the cost of a tremendous personal effort.

Even more fundamental than this, however, are the demoralizing and humiliating effects upon the self of continuously being treated charitably. The blind person comes to feel that he is not completely accepted as a mature, responsible person. As a second-class citizen, he must deal with the eroding sense of inadequacy that inevitably accompanies that status. Incidentally, it is important to note that this problem does not stem from the preconceptions others have about blindness; it is an effect of introducing the factor of blindness into the equation which describes the mechanics of interpersonal conduct.

There is one condition under which a blind person is able to escape this dilemma—the possession of a valued quality, trait, or attribute that he can use to compensate for his blindness. It is no accident that the blind persons who become most completely integrated into the larger society possess wealth, fame, or exceptional talent. These people can exchange prestige or money for the favors they must accept in order to function in daily life. They are unusual. A majority of blind people are elderly and poor, two traits that also have very low potential attractiveness to others.

In summary, four features of personal relationships affect the socialization of the blind. These are (1) the stereotyped beliefs that those who see bring to the interaction; (2) the fact that blindness is a stigma; (3) the fact that the conduct of such interactions is profoundly disturbed when one of the actors to the encounter cannot see; and (4) the fact that, by their nature, these are relationships of social dependency. The first two factors affect socialization outcomes in two ways; they force the blind man to recognize that he is a different, and lesser, person and they create a social identity that he either internalizes as a part of his self-concept or reacts to by rejecting. The stereotyped beliefs and the stigma, being contingencies no blind man can ignore, impose certain uniform behavioral patterns on those whom society labels blind.

The last two factors, which relate to the mechanics of interpersonal conduct, affect socialization outcomes in three ways; they force upon blind people further evidence of their difference; they deny them the kind of honest, uncluttered feedback about self that is commonplace to the sighted; and they place them in a subordinate position, making it difficult for them to form intimate relationships with those they regard as their intellectual and psychological equals. Together, these processes feed on one another and, from the initial heterogeneity of the blindness population, homogeneous patterns begin to emerge.

CHAPTER 3

Who Are the Blind?

IN everyday parlance, the term "blind" means "sightless." In work for the blind, this term refers to both sightless people and sighted people whose vision is seriously impaired. The problem of constructing a definition of blindness revolves around the question of where to draw a line among those with impaired vision.

THE DEFINITION OF BLINDNESS

Traditionally, ophthalmologists and other eye specialists have regarded the "form sense" as the essence of vision. The form sense, or visual acuity, is a measurement of the smallest retinal image that can be appreciated by the human eye. This measurement is expressed as a fraction, the numerator being the distance at which a given object can be seen by an individual, and the denominator being the distance at which that object would be seen if vision were normal. The most commonly used test of visual acuity was developed by Herman Snellen in 1868.[1] He varied the size of the object observed and held distance constant at 20 feet. The numerator of the fraction that expresses visual acuity is, therefore, always 20. What is called "normal" vision is expressed by the fraction 20/20, i.e., the ability to see at 20 feet an object that can be seen at 20 feet by a normal eye. A Snellen chart ordinarily consists of nine lines that contain letters of gradually diminishing size. The largest letter is equivalent to the fraction 20/200, i.e., the ability to see only at 20 feet what the "normal" eye is able to see at 200 feet. The remaining levels of visual acuity that can be measured by the average Snellen chart are 20/100, 20/70, 20/50, 20/40, 20/30, 20/20, 20/15, and 20/10.

In addition, normal vision, as it was defined by Snellen, was based upon measurement of "the minimum visual angle." This refers to the minimum angle formed by the convergence of light rays by the lens that is necessary for the eye to distinguish between two objects. Snellen's research shows that the minimum angle at which vision could take place was the equivalent of one minute of the arc of a circle (1/60 of a degree). The letter on Snellen's chart that measures the ability to focus to the minimum visual angle was constructed by projecting one minute of arc to a rectangle, and constructing a letter congruent with that rectangle. This letter was then adjusted to the distance of 20 feet and became the standard by which normal vision was measured.

The definition most often used for the purpose of determining eligibility for services to the blind is: "Central visual acuity of 20/200 or less in the better eye, with correcting lenses; or central visual acuity of more than 20/200 if there is a field defect in which the peripheral field has contracted to such an extent that the widest diameter of visual field represents an angular distance no greater than 20 degrees."[2]

[1] Herman Snellen, *Test-Types for the Determination of the Acuteness of Vision*, Publisher Utrecht, 1868.

[2] *Facts and Figures about Blindness*, American Foundation for the Blind, New York, 1967.

This definition has been severely criticized.[3] It has been pointed out that while form sense and the resolving power of the lens are the salient variabls in the area of normal vision, they are only two of many salient variables in the area of severe visual impairment. Others include the state of light adaptation of the eye, fatigue, illumination, contrast, reflection, systemic and eye pathology, the transparency of the media, the degree of refractive error, the degree of diffraction, the state of accommodation and convergence of the eye, the state of muscle function, and the adequacy of the scanning movement of the eye.[4] None of these factors is measured by the Snellen test.

Furthermore, as a measure of impaired vision, the Snellen chart is imprecise. On the standard Snellen chart there are finer gradients of visual acuity around the standard for normal than there are in the area of severe vision impairment. In fact, because of the way most Snellen charts are graduated, persons are classified as blind if their corrected vision is poorer than 20/100, rather than 20/200 or worse, as prescribed by the currently accepted administrative definition. On most Snellen charts there are no gradations between 20/200 and 20/100. If a person is unable to read the letter corresponding to 20/100 but able to read the letter corresponding to 20/200, he is classified 20/200. As a rule, no effort is made to determine whether he can read a letter corresponding to 20/190, 20/150, or 20/125. Since visual acuity as determined by the standard Snellen chart is widely accepted as definitive evidence of blindness, and since few organizations for the blind attempt to refine measures of visual acuity beyond those determined by the Snellen methods, the blind population includes an unknown number of persons who in fact are not blind by the criterion stipulated in the accepted definition.

There are other major objections to this definition. Perhaps the

[3] See Milton D. Graham, "Toward a Functional Definition of Blindness," *Research Bulletin*, American Foundation for the Blind, New York, No. 3, 1963, pp. 130–133, and Richard E. Hoover, "Visual Efficiency as a Criterion of Service Needs," *Research Bulletin*, American Foundation for the Blind, New York, No. 3, 1963, pp. 116–119.
[4] Hoover, *op. cit.*

most serious is that the demarcation line it sets between blindness and severe vision impairment is a completely arbitrary, indeed a capricious, one. There are no *a priori* theoretical, logical, or practical grounds by which to justify calling blind those people with visual acuity of 20/200 or worse. Nothing in the nature of Snellen's measure suggests that we must designate as significant the demarcation this definition makes between 20/100 and 20/200 vision. There is no evidence to suggest that the amount of the difference between these two degrees of visual acuity is any greater or more meaningful than are the differences between the 20/75 and the 20/100 levels, or between the 20/200 and the 20/400 levels. Moreover, there is little evidence that people who measure 20/200 on a Snellen chart have less functional vision than those who measure 20/100 on it. In short, the current definition of blindness is based upon a meaningless demarcation among those with severely impaired vision.

Since most of these criticisms are clearly justified, we are led to the conclusion that the currently accepted administrative definition of blindness is a crude and imprecise method of categorizing people who have severe loss of vision. It is insensitive to most of the important determinants of their functional vision; it arbitrarily excludes people with nearly similar levels of visual acuity; and it lumps together people who are totally blind and people who have a substantial amount of vision. People to whom the label of blindness is given are, therefore, extremely diversified, and the blindness population this definition creates is a heterogeneous one. It is important to keep this fact in mind as we review and interpret what is known about the population formed by the currently accepted administrative definition of blindness. However, the significance of this fact does not end here; it goes beyond to the heart of the issues raised in this book. The overwhelming majority of people who are classified as blind according to this definition can, in fact, see. All major prevalence estimates of blindness show that all but a small percentage of people who are "blind" have at least some measureable visual acuity, and that a plurality of them are in the category of 20/200.

Thus, most of those who undergo the socialization experiences that I will describe are not sightless; they are sighted people who experience difficulty seeing. The strength of this socialization process is suggested by the fact that people who can see come to behave as though they cannot, and that from so heterogeneous a population such homogeneity is eventually created.

THE BLINDNESS POPULATION OF THE UNITED STATES

At the present time, the number of blind people in the United States population is unknown. Accurate information about the incidence of blindness is extremely difficult to obtain. Blindness is comparatively rare in our population, and its identification is especially difficult because of the discouragingly particularistic administrative definition of the term. There is no regularly updated and complete nation-wide census of the blind, nor are complete administrative or other records kept on any substantial portion of the blindness population. These gaps complicate the task of describing the blindness population. We are forced to rely upon the *estimates* of the prevalence of blindness that have been made in four major recent studies. Each of these studies contains such major methodological deficiencies that it is hazardous to place much stock in its findings. All we can do is compare the findings of all four to determine whether there is any agreement concerning the size and composition of the blindness population.

Three of the four studies are based upon the case-finding method, in which an entire population or a representative sample of it has been screened for instances of blindness; the fourth is based upon data from registers for the blind, which are lists of persons who have been reported as blind to state commissioners for the blind. The three prevalence-estimates reports based upon the case-finding method were conducted as a part of the National Health Survey. The first report estimates the prevalence of blindness for the civilian, noninstitutional population of the United States for the time period

July 1957 to June 1958.[5] The data upon which these estimates are based come from interviews conducted in a representative sample of 36,000 households comprising 115,000 persons. In this study, persons over 6 years of age were considered blind if they were unable to read ordinary newspaper print with glasses; persons under 6 years of age were considered blind if a parent or guardian reported them as blind or as having no useful vision. A person was considered to have "other visual impairments" if he was blind in only one eye, or if he had visual difficulties in one or both eyes but was able to read ordinary newsprint.This study is ordinarily referred to as the "B-9" report on visual impairment.

The second report estimates the prevalence of blindness in the civilian, noninstitutional population of the United States for the two-year period July 1959 to June 1961.[6] These data were obtained from interviews of a sample of approximately 76,000 households comprising about 250,000 persons. This study, which is usually referred to as the "B-35" report, identified two types of visual impairments. The first, termed "severe visual impairments," is defined in the same way that the term "blindness" was defined in the B-9 study, i.e., inability to read ordinary newsprint even with the aid of glasses. The second category of impairment, referred to as "other visual impairments," is coextensive with that category in the B-9 study.

These studies are nation-wide estimates of the prevalence of *visual impairment,* not of blindness as that term is defined in administrative regulations. A question arises concerning the relationship between visual acuity of 20/200 or less and inability to read ordinary newsprint. While there are no conclusive data, presumptive evidence from the study by Eric Josephson and Marvin B. Sussman of the amount of visual impairment in Cleveland indicates that the relationship is not a direct one. They found that among those who were blind by the standard administrative definition of the term, 100 percent were unable to read newsprint; how-

[5] *Impairments by Type, Sex and Age: United States July 1957–June 1958,* U.S. Public Health Service, Washington, D.C., Series B-9, 1959. Hereafter referred to as the B-9 report.

[6] *Selected Impairments by Etiology and Activity Limitation: United States, July 1959–June 1961,* U.S. Public Health Service, Washington, D.C., Series B, No. 35, 1962. Hereafter referred to as the B-35 report.

ever, 62 percent of those who said that they could not read news-print were not blind by the accepted definition, and slightly more than one-quarter of them had vision of 20/40 or better.[7] These figures suggest that the prevalence estimates of visual impairments based upon the data of the National Health Survey are substantially greater than they would have been had the currently accepted administrative definition of blindness been employed as the basis for determining blindness in these studies.

The third report of the U.S. Public Health Service attempts to describe the distribution of binocular visual acuity in the civilian, noninstitutional population of the United States, 18 through 79 years of age.[8] The data, which cover the time period 1960–1962, are based upon interviews with, and examinations of, a sample of 6,672 persons. Central visual acuity for both distance and near vision was measured for each person by means of a sight screener, a device that adopts clinical measures of visual acuity for survey research programs.[9] The study reports the estimated distribution of binocular visual acuity in the specified population, including the number of people with visual acuities of 20/200 or less, i.e., the "legally" blind. The data of this report, which will be referred to as the "Binocular Visual Acuity report," are the closest available to prevalence estimates of blindness as that term is defined in administrative regulations. Unfortunately, there are two sources of error in this study. First, there are the normal errors of sampling and nonresponse that occur in any survey study. It has been calculated that, as a result of these errors, the estimates of this study may be off by not more than 2 percent.[10] The second source of error comes from the fact that in an undetermined number of examinations, persons with visual acuities poorer than 20/200 without correction did not have their glasses with them. When this was the case, the investigators considered the uncorrected acuity and the corrected acuity to be

[7] Eric Josephson and Marvin B. Sussman, "A Pilot Study of Visual Impairment," American Foundation for the Blind, New York, 1965, mimeographed.

[8] *Binocular Visual Acuity of Adults, United States, 1960–1962*, U.S. Public Health Service, Washington, D.C., Series 11, No. 3, 1964. Hereafter referred to as the Binocular Visual Acuity report.

[9] *Comparison of Two Vision-Testing Devices*, National Center for Health Statistics, Washington, D.C., Series 2, No. 1, 1963.

[10] Binocular Visual Acuity report, p. 26.

46

identical and reported them as such in the actual estimates. The effect of this procedure is, of course, to increase the estimate of the number who are blind by the administrative definition. As a result, the figures of this survey probably overestimate the true prevalence of blindness.

The fourth set of prevalence estimates of blindness was made by Ralph G. Hurlin for the years 1940, 1952, and 1960.[11] For a number of reasons it was believed that the most complete register for the blind was maintained by the state of North Carolina. Hurlin used the total number of persons on the North Carolina register as the basis for computing estimates for all other states and for the entire country. He made two assumptions: that the rate of blindness would vary from state to state, and the rate for each state would be determined chiefly by the composition of its population with respect to age, race, and public health standards. After each of these factors was weighted, scores were computed for all other states. By applying the data on blindness from the North Carolina register to other states, he was therefore able to generate estimates of the prevalence of blindness for the entire country.

There are obvious limitations to this kind of extrapolation. In this case, one source of error, which has an important bearing on our interpretation of Hurlin's findings, derives from the assumption that the North Carolina register for the blind was a complete count of blind persons in the state. In 1960, the North Carolina State Commission for the Blind reported that there were 12,432 blind persons on its register.[12] Hurlin believed that the register for that year was approximately complete and used it as the basis for his projections. Recently, this register has been re-examined and updated; as a result of this re-examination, the 1965 North Carolina register contains only 10,114 persons, or a drop of slightly over 2,200 people since

---

[11] Ralph G. Hurlin, "Estimated Prevalence of Blindness in the United States," *Social Security Bulletin*, Vol. 8, No. 3, 1945, pp. 17–22; "Estimated Prevalence of Blindness in the United States," *New Outlook for the Blind*, Vol. 47, No. 7, 1953, pp. 189–196; "Estimated Prevalence of Blindness in the United States and in Individual States, 1960," *Sight-Saving Review*, Vol. 32, No. 1, 1962.

[12] Hurlin 1962, *op. cit.*, p. 10.

1960.[13] From these data we conclude that the 1960 register contained the names of many persons who had died, moved, or were no longer blind, and that, consequently, the claim that it was complete was premature. In view of the fact that the 1960 figures are so critical to Hurlin's projections, we can conclude that he has overstated the prevalence of blindness that is recorded in registers for the blind.

This brief look at the methods used in each of the four principal prevalence estimates of blindness serves to alert us even more to the fact that it is impossible to make definitive estimates from them about the size and characteristics of the blindness population in the United States. Because the Binocular Visual Acuity report is the only one that used the currently accepted administrative definition of blindness on a sample of adults who were drawn at random from the United States population, we will use it as the standard against which to compare findings of the other three studies.

Amount of Blindness

According to the Binocular Visual Acuity study, for the period 1960–1962 there were an estimated 889,000 blind people between the ages of 18 and 79 in the noninstitutional population of the United States.[14] By applying this figure to the comparable United States population for 1965, we can estimate that there are now about 900,000 blind people. Fifty-three percent of them have a corrected visual acuity poorer than 20/200; the remaining 47 percent have a corrected acuity of 20/200.

These figures exclude three major groups: children under 18 years of age, persons who are in institutions, and persons 80 years of age and older.

According to the 1965 census of the American Printing House for the Blind, there are 18,093 school-age children in the United States who are blind.[15] This figure, which covers the age group 6 to

[13] *The Model Reporting Area for Blindness Statistics*, National Institute of Neurological Diseases and Blindness, Washington, D.C., p. 3.

[14] Binocular Visual Acuity report, p. 16.

[15] *Annual Report*, American Printing House for the Blind, Louisville, Ky., 1965.

21, overlaps slightly with estimates of the Binocular Visual Acuity report for the age group 18 to 24. No definitive data are available on the number of children of preschool age who are blind. A rule of thumb that has been adopted by many educators and specialists on blind children is that the school-age children make up about two-thirds of the total population of blind children, and that preschool children account for the remaining one-third. If we adopt this rule, it can be estimated that there are approximately 27,000 blind children under the age of 21. This figure is probably an underestimation. William D. Simmons located in California mental hospitals more blind children than had been estimated for the whole state.[16] Since his study has not been replicated in other states, it is not possible to take its findings as representative of the amount of underestimation of the total population of blind children in the United States. I will therefore rely upon the figure of 27,000, recognizing that it is probably conservative.

The number of blind persons in institutions in the United States is undetermined. The only available data are for two types of institutions in which the largest number of blind persons are most likely to be found—long-stay mental hospitals and institutions for the aged and chronically ill. Two reports by the National Center for Health Statistics on these institutions provide a reasonable basis for estimating the amount of blindness in the institutionalized population of the United States. According to these reports, there are 6,143 totally blind persons in long-term mental hospitals,[17] and 17,178 totally blind persons in institutions for the aged and chronically ill.[18] In each study, an attempt was also made to estimate the number of persons with "serious visual problems." A person was so cate-

[16] William D. Simmons, "A Survey of Blind, Severely Visually Impaired, and Multiply-Handicapped Children in California: A Preliminary Report," *Proceedings of the West Coast Regional Conference on Research Related to Blind and Severely Visually Impaired Children*, American Foundation for the Blind, New York, 1965, pp. 11–15.

[17] *Characteristics of Patients in Mental Hospitals, United States, April–June, 1963*, National Center for Health Statistics, Washington, D.C., Series 12, No. 3, 1965, pp. 20–21.

[18] *Characteristics of Residents in Institutions for the Aged and Chronically Ill, United States, April–June, 1963*, National Center for Health Statistics, Washington, D.C., 1965, p. 27.

gorized if he had serious difficulty seeing even with the aid of glasses. Some persons who were legally blind, but not totally blind, undoubtedly fell into this category. The studies estimate that there are 18,839 persons with serious visual problems in mental hospitals, and 80,839 such persons in institutions for the aged and chronically ill. On the basis of these figures, we can estimate that there are about 23,000 totally blind persons in these two types of institutions, and an additional 99,000 persons with serious visual problems.

Finally, no data are available on the number of blind persons over the age of 80. The prevalence of blindness in this segment of the population can be estimated if the assumption is made that the blindness rate per 1,000 of the population for persons 80 years of age and older is at least as high as it is for those in the age range 75 to 79. According to the Binocular Visual Acuity report, this blindness rate is 33 per 1,000.[19] In 1965, there were approximately 3,000,000 noninstitutionalized persons 80 years of age or older. We can therefore calculate that there are about 99,000 legally blind persons in this segment of the population.

From these figures we can estimate that there are slightly over one million blind people in the United States at the present time. This estimate is in general agreement with the findings of both the B-9 and B-35 reports of visual impairment. In the B-9 study, which applies to the time period July 1957–June 1958, it was estimated that there were 960,000 severely visually impaired persons in the civilian noninstitutional population of the continental United States.[20] The B-35 study, which applies to the period July 1959 to June 1961, estimated that there were 988,000 persons with severe visual impairments.[21] When we apply these figures to the comparable United States population for 1965, we derive an estimate that is almost exactly the same as the one based on the Binocular Visual Acuity report.

The Hurlin figures, which are based upon an extrapolation of data from one state register to the entire country, are substantially

[19] Binocular Visual Acuity report, p. 16.
[20] B-9 report, p. 11.
[21] B-35 report, p. 5.

lower than the findings of these other three studies. Hurlin estimated that in 1960 there were about 385,000 blind people in the United States.[22] By applying his blindness rate of 2.14 per 1,000 to the 1965 census figures, he estimates that there are now about 420,000 persons in the blindness population.

From these various figures we are lead to the preposterous conclusion that there are between 400,000 and 1,000,000 blind people in the United States at the present time. The three National Health Survey reports seem to agree on the latter figure; the Hurlin estimates stand alone on the former figure. While there are major errors in all four studies, those in the Hurlin method seem more glaring than those in the National Health Survey reports. For this reason, I am inclined toward the conclusion that the larger figure is closer than the smaller figure to the true prevalence rate of blindness.

The Relationship between Age and Blindness

Data of the Binocular Visual Acuity report indicate that blindness is most often found among older persons. According to this report, 46 percent of persons who are legally blind are between the ages of 65 and 79; and 21 percent are 55 to 64 years of age.[23] Consequently, 67 percent of the blind population are in age groups in which retirement is either imminent or a reality. Conversely, only a small number of the blind are young persons; only about 18 percent of the total estimated cases of blindness are found among persons 18 to 44.

The strong association between age and blindness is demonstrated in another way—the age-specific rates per thousand of the population, shown in the accompanying table. If we use the estimates for the amount of blindness in children presented in the preceding section, we can estimate that the blindness rate for persons under 21 is only about .35. These data show in a striking fashion that the large majority of cases of blindness occur in older persons.

The data of the Binocular Visual Acuity report suggest another

[22] Hurlin 1962, *op. cit.*, p. 4.
[23] Binocular Visual Acuity report, p. 16.

Blindness Rate per Thousand Population

Age Group	Rate
18–24	2.9
25–34	2.6
35–44	2.3
45–54	6.7
55–64	12.0
65–74	28.0
75–79	33.0

Source: *Binocular Visual Acuity of Adults, United States, 1960–1962*, U.S. Public Health Service, Washington, D.C., Series 11, No. 3, 1964, p. 16.

fact about the relationship between age and blindness; older blind persons tend to be more severely impaired than younger blind persons. Sixty-seven percent of blind persons in the age bracket 65 to 74 have visual acuity poorer than 20/200; 60 percent of those 75 to 79 have a similar acuity. By contrast, only 36 percent of blind persons 18 to 24 have visual acuities poorer than 20/200; and only 26 percent of blind persons 25 to 34 have vision poorer than 20/200.[24] From these data we can conclude that the visual impairment that occurs in older persons tends to be more severe than the visual impairment that occurs in the young.

The findings of the B-9, B-35, and Hurlin reports regarding the relationship of age and blindness agree with the findings of the Binocular Visual Acuity report. The B-9 study found that 67 percent of persons who were blind (i.e., couldn't read ordinary newsprint) were 65 or older; 21 percent were between the ages of 45 and 64; and only 12 percent were in the younger age groups.[25] The findings of the B-35 study with respect to age and blindness are almost identical.[26] Hurlin found that 46 percent of persons on the North Carolina state register for the blind were 65 or older; 24 percent were 45 to 64; 19 percent were between the ages of 19 and 44; and the remaining 11

[24] *Ibid.*
[25] B-9 report, p. 11.
[26] B-35 report, p. 5.

percent were children 18 or younger.[27] While the findings of the Hurlin study with respect to the association of age and blindness are generally similar to the findings of the other reports, the magnitude of the association he reports is not so great. Finally, the findings of the B-9 and the B-35 studies also show that older persons who are visually impaired tend to have more severe impairments than younger persons who are impaired.

The four prevalence estimates of blindness all agree, then, that blindness occurs most commonly in older persons, that it is comparatively uncommon in adults of employment age, that it can be described as a rare condition in children, and that the degree of vision loss older persons have suffered appears to be more severe than that found among the young.

The Relationship Between Sex and Blindness

The data of the Binocular Visual Acuity report indicate that blindness is more commonly found in women than in men. Sixty-nine percent of persons with visual acuity of 20/200 or less were women. This report also indicates that women who are blind are likely to have more severe impairment of vision than men who are blind. Whereas almost 40 percent of those who have an acuity of 20/200 were men, only 23 percent of those with an acuity poorer than 20/200 were men.[28] These data should be interpreted cautiously in view of the fact that the relative sampling error for men is quite large.

The data of the B-9 and B-35 studies are consistent with these findings, although the magnitude of the sex difference is not quite so high. The B-9 study found that about 40 percent of the cases of blindness were in men;[29] the comparable figure for the B-35 report was 43 percent.[30] The Hurlin study reports a sex difference, but its

[27] Hurlin 1962, *op. cit.*, pp. 5–6.
[28] Binocular Visual Acuity report, p. 16.
[29] B-9 report, p. 10.
[30] B-35 report, p. 6.

magnitude is significantly smaller than in any of the other studies. He reports that about 49 percent of all cases of blindness on the North Carolina register were men.[31]

The Relationships Among Age, Sex, and Blindness

In view of the fact that longevity is greater for women than for men, it is possible that the relationship between sex and blindness is in reality an index of the relationship of blindness to age. In order to determine whether this is correct, I examined the relationships between sex and blindness with age held constant. Relevant available data are inadequate, for several reasons. The sampling error for certain age categories of men is too high to place confidence in some of the specific age and sex estimates of the Binocular Visual Acuity report; the B-9 study does not report data on this relationship at all; and the data of the B-35 study have combined several age categories. Any conclusions drawn from the data of these studies are consequently subject to a good deal of error.

The findings of the Binocular Visual Acuity report indicate that the prevalence rate of blindness is higher in all age categories for females than for males. In all age groups 45 and over, the prevalence rates for blindness among women are roughly double those for men; among persons 44 years of age and younger, there is an important but smaller difference.[32] The latter figure is difficult to interpret, however, because the greatest sampling error occurred among men in this age group.

The findings of the B-35 study indicate that the prevalence rates of severe visual impairment for persons under 65 do not differ by sex; for those over 65, the blindness rate is 47 for women and 38 for men.[33] However, it is difficult to determine if these data contradict the findings of the Binocular Visual Acuity report because it is impossible to compute specific age-prevalence rates for men and women under 65 years of age.

[31] Hurlin 1962, *op. cit.*, p. 10.
[32] Binocular Visual Acuity report, p. 16.
[33] B-35 report, p. 6.

Although no clear conclusions can be drawn regarding the relationships of sex and blindness, it is possible to describe each age-sex segment of the population in terms of its proportionate contribution to the total population of the persons with severely impaired vision. The largest segment of the blind population consists of women 55 years of age and older; there are more blind women 18 to 54 than there are blind men 55 and older; and only about 12 percent of this entire blind population are men of employable age.

The data of the B-35 report indicate that 4 out of 10 cases of blindness occur in women 65 and older; another 3 out of 10 cases are men 65 and older; and the proportionate contribution of men and women under 65 is approximately equal (about 16.5 percent for each group).[34]

From these figures we conclude that women 55 and older account for about 50 percent of all cases of blindness, that there are more blind women 18 to 54 than there are blind men 65 to 79, and that blind men 18 to 54 account for only about 13 percent of the total blindness population.

The Relationship Between Race and Blindness

The Hurlin estimates are the only available figures on the relationship between racial background and blindness. He found that the rate of blindness for whites in North Carolina was 2.25 per thousand; the comparable rate for nonwhites was 4.11.[35] The applicability of these figures to other sections of this country is, of course, undetermined.

Summary

Taken collectively, the data of these various studies suggest that the nearly one million blind people in the United States can be subdivided into four groups. The first group consists of the aged blind. It includes all people over the age of 65 who are blind according to

[34] *Ibid.*
[35] Hurlin 1962, *op. cit.*, p. 10.

the currently accepted administrative definition of blindness. All prevalence estimates studies agree that the aged blind comprise the largest subgroup of the blindness population, slightly over two-thirds of all the blind. The second category consists of blind people whose characteristics, including blindness, either place them out of the labor force, or tend to make employment extremely difficult for them. This group, which I will call "non-aged unemployable adults," includes blind people who have little education and few useful skills, those who are multiply handicapped, and women for whom employment is not normally expected. While the precise proportion of the blindness population that falls into this group is unknown, it probably amounts to no more than 10 to 15 percent of it. The third group are non-aged adults who are potentially employable. Persons in this group are predominantly males, most of whom have no major handicaps other than blindness. Like the previous group, their numbers probably do not exceed 10 to 15 percent of the total blindness population. The fourth group are blind children, of whom there are about 27,000. As such, they represent only about 2 to 3 percent of the total blindness population.

These four groups can be subdivided into those whose only disability is blindness and those who are multiply handicapped. Exact figures on the proportion of each group who are multiply handicapped are available only for children;[36] however, it is probably the case that substantial numbers of persons in all subgroups, except non-aged employable adults, are multiply handicapped.

[36] Milton D. Graham, *Multiply Impaired Blind Children: A National Problem*, American Foundation for the Blind, New York, 1968.

CHAPTER 4

The Selection of Clients from

the Blind Population

Not all people who are classified as blind according to the currently accepted administrative definition of the term become clients of organizations in the blindness system. Clients of agencies for the blind comprise only a small proportion of the total blindness population, and they are representative of only a highly selective segment of it. Unfortunately, few organizations for the blind maintain reliable data on the numbers and characteristics of those they serve, so that it is impossible to make direct comparisons between the characteristics of blind people who are served and those of the total blind population. The alternative, somewhat cumbersome procedure that I have had to use involves an analysis of the types of services available to blind people through the blindness system, and of the way the resources of this system are differentially allocated to each type of service. From such analysis it is possible to make inferences about the appropriateness to each subgroup of the blind population of the services offered.

TYPES OF SERVICES IN THE BLINDNESS SYSTEM

The services offered to blind people through the blindness system fall into five basic categories: support services; instrumental services; rehabilitation and vocational services; children's services; and vision-enhancement, prevention of blindness, and eye-treatment programs.[1]

Support Services

In the broadest sense, support services include activities designed to maintain individuals at least at a minimal level of existence. Two different types of support services are offered: income-maintenance programs, which provide direct financial support either to the blind person or to his family, and personal-care programs, which provide the client with a wide spectrum of services, ranging from those essential for survival to those held to be essential for a happy fulfilled existence. Examples of the former are provision of food, shelter, clothing, and minimal health care. Examples of the latter are recreation, social contacts, psycho-social help, and help with communication skills. Occasionally, such services are offered through ordinary agencies for the blind; by and large, however, they are provided in custodial settings.

Support services are relevant to all blind people at some point immediately following the onset of blindness. Among at least some segments of the blindness population, the need for support services probably diminishes as other activities, such as instrumental and rehabilitation services, vocational services, and education become effective. Because such non-support services apply to only a fraction of the total blind population, however, support services must be provided to many blind people on an indefinite basis. The constituencies of the blind for whom such services are most likely to be required

[1] This classification of services to the blind is borrowed from a report on the blindness system by the Organization for Social and Technical Innovation (OSTI). See "An Analysis of Blindness and Services to the Blind in the United States," OSTI, Boston, 1967, mimeographed.

continuously are the aged blind, non-aged unemployable adults, and multiply handicapped blind people in all age groups.

Instrumental Services

Instrumental services consist of activities intended to make blind people independent in the areas of work, education, and the routines of everyday life. Although these services are instrumental in helping the blind person with problems in each of these areas, they are not specifically designed for any one of them. The major types of instrumental services are training in the use of mobility devices, such as guide dogs and canes; training in the use of braille or special recording equipment, such as talking-book machines and tape recorders; and training in the skills required to perform the basic activities of everyday life. As a rule, instrumental services are not the province of any one type of agency or program; rather, they are a part of the standard repertoire of services that are offered to the blind by many organizations for the blind. Almost all blind people require instrumental services following the onset of their disability, and many of them continue to receive such services indefinitely.

Rehabilitation and Vocational Services

This category includes services oriented to preparation for and securing of employment for the blind. Rehabilitation and vocational services cover a wide spectrum of activities, including initial evaluations of a client to determine his ability to work; rehabilitation services aimed at restoring basic losses that result from blindness; counseling to prepare him for the job he is deemed best suited to perform; training for that job; training in the use of special work-related devices; placement in industrial or other competitive employment situations; or, when competitive employment is impossible, location of a job for him in a special program such as a sheltered workship or a vending stand. Since most organizations require tangible evidence that employment is a feasible objective before a client can qualify for these services, rehabilitation and vocational services are given almost entirely to non-aged employable adults.

Children's Services

These refer to the education of blind children as well as to instrumental services and other rehabilitative activities that enable such children to attain their educational goals. Children's services include counseling of blind children and their parents; training in the use of braille, canes, and other equipment that may increase the child's ability to cope with the educational process; and recreational and other organized leisure-time activities. The educational settings are of two types: residential schools that specialize in the education of blind children and programs of special education within the public school system that enable blind children to attend primary and secondary schools in their home communities.

Vision-Enhancement, Prevention-of-Blindness, and Medical Eye-Treatment Services

Vision-enhancement programs are designed to improve residual vision among visually impaired people who are not totally blind and to deter the loss of what vision remains. Such programs are of potential use to all legally blind people except the totally blind. Prevention-of-blindness programs are aimed at deterring the rate of flow of people from the sighted population into the population of the legally blind. Medical eye-treatment programs are relevant for those whose blindness is the result of a condition that may respond to medical care. By and large, these programs are situated in ordinary medical facilities and are therefore outside of the blindness system.

This classification of services for the blind is suggested in part by the nature of the services provided and in part by the organizational system by which such services are delivered to the blind population. Because of certain features of this organizational delivery system, there is overlap between a number of the services I have identified. It is not always easy or even possible to draw a line between personal-care and instrumental services, or between instrumental services and rehabilitation. It is important to keep this fact in mind in evaluating information about the differential allocation of the resources of the blindness system to these various service functions.

THE ALLOCATION OF RESOURCES IN THE BLINDNESS SYSTEM

The resources of the blindness system can be divided into three basic categories—manpower resources, financial resources, and resources in the form of an organizational delivery system for services. Unfortunately, there is very little information on manpower resources in work for the blind. A substantial, yet incomplete, amount of information is available, however, concerning both organizations for the blind and financial expenditures in this field. My analysis of resource allocations to the different service functions of work for the blind is therefore based upon data I have collected about these two types of resources.

At the outset, it is important to understand a number of features of what I am calling "the blindness system." It is incorrect to speak of organizations and programs for the blind as constituting a social welfare system. A system implies a regularly interacting, interdependent group of units that together form a unified whole. The organizations and programs comprising the field of work for the blind were not born out of a master plan, nor are their current activities guided by any commonly held conceptions about the total welfare problem of blindness in this country. Communication among organizations for the blind for the purpose of coordinating activities and allocating responsibilities for serving the various segments of the blind population is extremely limited, and monetary and manpower resources are not deliberately and explicitly allocated in accordance with the social and welfare needs of this population. Rather, organizations and programs for the blind are an aggregate of bureaucratic entities that share a common interest in the problems of blindness, but whose activities are not coordinated and integrated to any meaningful degree. It is merely for convenience that I use the phrase "blindness system" to refer to this aggregate of activities, programs, and organizations, which is not in fact a system.

The number of programs and agencies that comprise the organizational delivery system of services for the blind in America is very large.[2] In all, I have been able to identify a total of 803 separate agen-

[2] *Directory of Agencies Serving Blind Persons in the United States*, 15th ed., American Foundation for the Blind, New York, 1967.

cies, organizations, and programs for the blind in the United States.[3] This means that there is one blindness facility for about every 1,000 blind people in this country. It is estimated that the more than 800 agencies annually spend about $470,000,000; this amounts to an annual expenditure of about $500 for every man, woman, and child in the United States who is blind. As we shall see, the blindness system serves only a minority of all blind people. As a result, the ratio of agencies to clients is probably a good deal lower, and the per capita expenditures a good deal higher, than the figures I have reported here.

How are these resources allocated among the service functions of the blindness system? A partial answer to this question can be obtained by matching organizations and financial expenditures with each of the five separate functions.

Support Services

The largest single investment of financial resources of the blindness system goes for income maintenance. Three such programs exist: Aid to the Needy Blind; Old-Age, Survivors and Disability Insurance; and the Veterans' Administration program for blinded veterans of the armed forces.[4] The first of these programs is jointly supported by the federal government and the participating states; the latter two are supported entirely by federal appropriations. The purpose of Aid to the Needy Blind is to provide assistance to blind people who have no means of support, or who are unable to remain self-sufficient even though employed. Eligibility for assistance under this program is based upon a means test, and the amount of assistance provided is quite modest. At the present time about 90,000 blind people are receiving aid through this program at an annual

[3] Robert A. Scott, "The Selection of Clients by Social Welfare Agencies: The Case of the Blind," *Social Problems*, Vol. 14, No. 3, 1967, pp. 248–257.
[4] A fourth type of income-maintenance program for the blind is the extra income tax exemption to which all legally blind persons are entitled. This program is omitted from my discussion because, at the time of publication, no data were available concerning the number of persons who claimed such an exemption.

cost of $100,800,000.[5] A recent study of recipients of aid from this program estimated that about 60 percent of them are men and women of working age who supplement their welfare assistance by working on a part-time or full-time basis in jobs specifically reserved for the blind.[6] The remainder are people over 65 whose income is inadequate for their needs.

Old-Age, Survivors and Disability Insurance is part of the social security program. It is designed to provide assistance to people of working age who are covered by social security and who become disabled. The program provides disabled people at the time at which they become disabled with the social security benefits they would otherwise have received when they retired. Because it is an insurance program, means tests are not required. Payments under this program, though greater than those provided under Aid to the Needy Blind, are nevertheless modest. In 1966, 60,000 blind people were receiving payments through this program; the total expenditure for that year came to $50,976,000.[7]

The Veterans' Administration provides direct financial payments to blind veterans of the armed forces. These payments are generous, particularly for those who lost their sight while on active duty. Benefits are determined by the extent of the disability and are uninfluenced by a veteran's subsequent income from employment. Recipients of aid under this program are mainly young and middle-aged persons, the overwhelming majority of whom have served in World War II and the Korean conflict. In 1966 the Veterans' Administration paid out a total of $116,423,688 to 89,225 veterans.[8]

In total, then, approximately $268,000,000 is given for direct financial assistance to about 240,000 blind people. The majority of these recipients are men and women under the age of 65. In evaluating this information, it is important to recognize that no data are available concerning the sources of income of blind people who are

---

[5] *Health, Education and Welfare Indicators*, January 1967.

[6] Robert H. Mugge, "Recipients of Aid to the Blind," *Welfare in Review*, April 1965.

[7] *Health, Education and Welfare Indicators*, October 1966.

[8] "An Analysis of Blindness and Services to the Blind in the United States," Appendix 3, p. 10.

65 years of age and older. It is fair to assume that many of them are receiving the standard social security benefits most aged people are entitled to receive when they retire.

It is extremely difficult to isolate the resources spent on personal-care services for the blind. This is partly because generic agencies such as hospitals, nursing homes, and domiciles provide care for all elderly and disabled people including the blind.[9] Also, some of the personal-care services provided within the blindness system are supplied by multifunctional agencies that do not itemize expenditures for this type of service. The reports I have obtained from the 21 domiciliary establishments that cater exclusively to elderly blind people indicate that they care for a total of about a thousand elderly and multiply-handicapped people.[10] According to the OSTI report on the blindness system, the total estimated expenditures on personal-care services for the blind amount to about $10,500,000.[11]

Instrumental Services

The amount of resources expended on instrumental services for the blind is difficult to estimate with any precision. Many instrumental services offered to the blind cannot be isolated from the larger programs of which they are a part. There are, however, three kinds of instrumental-service programs that can be separately identified. The first consists of public and private organizations that specialize in transcribing, publishing, recording, and distributing materials to the blind. The major publicly supported program in this area is administered through the Library of Congress and its 33 regional branches. This program, which is supported at both the federal and the state level, cost $8,600,000 in 1966.[12] There are

[9] *Characteristics of Patients in Mental Hospitals, United States, April–June, 1963*, National Center for Health Statistics, Washington, D.C., Series 12, No. 3, 1965, and *Characteristics of Residents in Institutions for the Aged and Chronically Ill, United States, April–June 1963*, National Center for Health Statistics, Washington, D.C., 1965.

[10] *Directory of Agencies Serving Blind Persons in the United States.*

[11] "An Analysis of Blindness and Services to the Blind in the United States," Chap. 2, p. 45.

[12] *Ibid.*, Appendix 3, p. 3.

also 25 private agencies for the blind specializing in this particular type of service.[13] According to the OSTI report, these organizations spend about $7,700,000 annually.[14] In total, then, about $16,300,000 is spent each year on this type of instrumental service.

The second main category of instrumental services are programs supported and administered by state commissions for the blind. These programs offer a fairly wide range of instrumental services to blind people of all ages. According to the OSTI report, total expenditures for this type of program amount to about $15,000,000 annually.[15]

The third category of instrumental programs that can be separately identified as such are guide-dog schools. There are eight such schools in the United States, all of which are privately supported. The OSTI report states that these schools spend about $2,600,000 each year.[16]

Over all, then, 66 organizations specialize in instrumental services for the blind. This figure excludes state commissions for the blind that offer instrumental services as a part of their comprehensive programs for blind people. We can estimate that about $31,000,000 is spent on instrumental-service functions in the blindness system.[17]

Rehabilitation and Vocational Services

More organizations in the blindness system are concerned exclusively with these functions than with any other type of service offered to the blind. In all, there are almost 400 agencies, organizations, and branch offices of federally coordinated programs that devote exclusive attention to this function. Sixty of these agencies are state-wide vocational rehabilitation administration offices, and another 257 are the local branch offices through which services are actually given. There are five rehabilitation centers for the blind and about

[13] *Directory of Agencies Serving Blind Persons in the United States*, p. 10.
[14] "An Analysis of Blindness and Services to the Blind in the United States," Appendix 3, p. 21.
[15] *Ibid.*, Appendix 3, p. 24.
[16] *Ibid.*, Appendix 3, p. 21.
[17] *Ibid.*

70 sheltered workshops. In addition, vocational training and employment of the blind are major, if not primary, concerns of nearly 80 other private agencies for the blind.[18]

It has been conservatively estimated that about $50,000,000 is spent annually on rehabilitation and vocational services.[19] The bulk of this money—about $30,000,000—comes from the Vocational Rehabilitation Administration. An additional $7,500,000 is supplied by states as matching funds for federal allocations. The OSTI report estimates that about $10,000,000 is spent annually by sheltered workshops for the blind and that the five private rehabilitation centers spend about $1,000,000 each year.[20] No estimates are available of how much is spent by other private agencies on rehabilitation and vocational services.

Children's Services

The education, rehabilitation, and care of blind children have always been dominant among the concerns of the field of work for the blind. In all there are about 136 different organizations or programs that specialize in some type of service for blind children. Most of them sponsor activities oriented to education. There are 55 residential schools for the blind and 50 special-education programs in which blind children are given the opportunity to attend public schools in their home communities. In 1966, 5,507 youngsters attended residential schools for the blind and 11,472 blind children were in public day-school programs. In that year, residential schools spent about $22,800,000 and public day-school programs spent about $25,135,000.[21] Two other organizations concerned with the education of blind children—The American Printing House for the Blind and the Office of Education—together spent about $6,500,000 on a variety of training, educational, and research projects for blind children.[22]

[18] *Directory of Agencies Serving Blind Persons in the United States.*
[19] "An Analysis of Blindness and Services to the Blind in the United States," Appendix 3, p. 24.
[20] *Ibid.*, Appendix 3, p. 21.
[21] *Ibid.*, Appendix 3, p. 16.
[22] *Ibid.*, Appendix 3, p. 24.

Twenty-nine privately sponsored agencies specialize in instrumental services for blind children. There are no complete data on the amount of money such organizations spend. On the basis of a small sample of them, the OSTI report estimates that such agencies probably spend about $4,500,000 each year on blind children.[23] This figure excludes the numerous programs for blind children that are a part of the over-all programs of most multifunctional agencies.

These figures indicate that the 136 organizations concerned with blind children spend a minimum of $59,000,000 each year on educational and instrumental services to blind children.

Vision-Enhancement, Prevention, and Medical-Treatment Services

While it is impossible to obtain exact figures on the amount of money spent on these service functions, it is probably the case that there are fewer resources allocated to these functions than to any of the other services I have described. The six organizations ,that are concerned specifically with the prevention of blindness spend about $3,500,000 annually.[24] Only one medical-treatment agency within the blindness system could be identified as such; its budget is about $300,000.[25] Most vision-enhancement programs are situated in large rehabilitation centers or in multifunctional agencies; it is therefore impossible to estimate how much is spent on them each year. According to the OSTI report, a total of about $4,000,000 is spent on enhancement of vision and prevention and cure of blindness in the blindness system each year.[26]

General Service Agencies

In this analysis I have identified 674 different agencies, organizations, and programs that place exclusive or primary emphasis on one of the five basic service functions in work for the blind. An addi-

[23] *Ibid.*, Appendix 3. p. 21.
[24] *Ibid.*
[25] *Ibid.*
[26] *Ibid.*, Appendix 3, p. 24.

tional 110 private agencies and 19 local public agencies perform more generalized functions for the blind.[27] The 110 private agencies can be broken down into six basic categories.

1. LARGE MULTIFUNCTIONAL AGENCIES FOR THE BLIND. Such agencies offer many services to blind people of all ages and are usually found only in the very large metropolitan areas of the country where a need and the necessary private resources for funding exist. A typical multifunctional agency maintains such programs as a nursery school for pre-school blind children; recreation and other programs for blind adolescents; rehabilitation services for blind people of all ages; psychological counseling and social casework or group-work services; a home teaching service; mobility instruction; a sheltered workshop and craftshop; domiciliary facilities; and a host of other services such as music education, reading services, volunteer services, transportation services, limited medical care, and, in the case of one agency, a special burial plot for its clients. While these agencies offer services to all groups of blind people, a majority of them place heavy, if not exclusive, emphasis on children and employable adults. There are 21 such agencies in the United States. The OSTI report estimates that the agencies spend about $26,000,000 each year.[28]

2. GENERAL SOCIAL WELFARE ORGANIZATIONS. These provide services for many groups of people, some of whom may be blind. Goodwill Industries, for example, will often reserve a few positions for blind people in their salvage shops. Of the 13 general organizations that serve blind people, most are sheltered workshops in which people with other handicaps also work. There is no way to determine how much money is spent just for blind people by such organizations.

3. SMALL GENERAL SERVICE AGENCIES FOR THE BLIND. These agencies attempt to pattern themselves after the larger multifunc-

[27] *Directory of Agencies Serving Blind Persons in the United States.*
[28] "An Analysis of Blindness and Services to the Blind in the United States," Appendix 3, p. 21.

tional agencies. As a rule, they are located in medium-sized metropolitan areas where there are likely to be only a few thousand blind persons at any given time. Because they lack the necessary financial and professional resources, the programs of such organizations are usually modest. Some rehabilitation services are provided; a few modest services for elderly people may be available; the parents of blind children are able to obtain some elementary counseling; and a "drop in" club is maintained in lieu of any formal recreational programs. I have been able to identify twelve such organizations in the blindness system; no data are available on their total expenditures.

4. LIMITED-FUNCTION ORGANIZATIONS FOR THE BLIND. These agencies specialize in providing a few kinds of services to particular groups of blind people. Some provide recreational and social activities to blind adults; some emphasize employment of adults in sheltered workshops and psychological-counseling programs for children; some stress employment and recreation for adults; others are domiciliary establishments. Agencies with limited functions are usually located in small or moderately populated urban areas, although organizations of this type are not unknown to the larger cities. Their resources are small, and their clientele in any given year seldom exceeds 150 to 200 persons. There are 33 such agencies. No data are available concerning the annual expenditures by such organizations.

5. OTHER BLINDNESS ORGANIZATIONS. Some organizations for the blind either offer services of a highly particularistic nature or engage in activities that cannot be subsumed under any of the other categories I have defined. These include such things as "paper organizations," which are created for administrative purposes; clinics in which severely visually impaired persons may obtain special lenses to aid them in reading or doing close work; special summer camps for blind children and adults; and employment services for the blind. Twenty-six organizations fall into this category. No data exist on the amount of resources spent each year by these organizations.

6. CONSULTING AGENCIES. These agencies usually do not provide any direct services; they exist for the purpose of representing the field, or some segment of it, to the government, Congress, or the local community. Such organizations operate as pressure groups that attempt to bring about changes within work for the blind by consulting with direct service agencies or by lobbying at the federal and state levels. In all there are five such agencies in the United States; no exact data are presently available on their expenditures.

In the OSTI report it is estimated that these 110 private agencies spend a total of about $47,500,000 each year.[29] Except for the separate estimates that have been made for large multifunctional agencies, it is not possible to itemize expenditures by the other types of agencies in this category.

The 19 local public organizations for the blind include branch offices of federal programs, such as the Old-Age, Survivors and Disability Insurance and certain publicly supported sheltered workshops for the blind.

THE SELECTION OF CLIENTS FROM THE BLINDNESS POPULATION

From this analysis of organizations and financial resources in the blindness system a number of conclusions can be drawn about the recruitment of clients from the blindness population. First, it appears that the services of a majority of organizations and programs for the blind are suitable for a small, highly selected portion of the blind population. Nearly two-thirds of these organizations cater exclusively to either children or non-aged adults; and at least 60 percent of all economic resources, exclusive of income maintenance, are earmarked for these two groups. Second, the blindness system provides very few services for the aged blind. A vast majority of recipients of payments from income-maintenance programs in the blindness system are non-aged adults. Other service programs from which the aged blind might benefit, such as personal care, instrumental services, vision enhancement, or sight restoration, receive

[29] *Ibid.*

less than 10 percent of all economic resources of this system and represent the primary function of only about one-tenth of all organizations and programs for the blind. Moreover, the majority of the 110 private agencies that offer a mix of services cater largely to children and to non-aged adults who are employable. While elderly people are not automatically ineligible for services in such organizations, services for them are usually appendages to programs for blind people in other age groups. Participation of the elderly in these programs therefore depends upon their having the same general level of health and stamina as those for whom the programs are primarily intended.

An additional fact is not apparent from these data. Programs for children and adults are not geared to serve all blind persons in a given age group. Numerous services are available for the child who is educable, but few for the multiply-handicapped child. There are many services for the blind person who is thought to be employable, but few for the one who is thought to be untrainable or for whom employment is an unrealistic goal. Since recreation programs for elderly blind persons are located in the agency itself, only those elderly blind people who are mobile and independent enough to travel can take advantage of them. (In short, programs are geared to serve selected blind people, usually those who enjoy the highest probability of success.)

It appears, then, that services for the blind are largely restricted to two of the five major constituencies of the blind—children and non-aged employable adults. Through basic processes of recruitment, most of the multiply handicapped, the uneducable, the untrainable, the unemployable, and the aged are screened out. Socialization experiences that occur in organizations for the blind are therefore reserved for a small, somewhat elite portion of all blind people. The recruitment processes by which some blind people are screened in and others screened out and the socialization experiences of clients of organizations for the blind are topics to which we shall now turn.

CHAPTER 5

The Socialization of the Blind

in Blindness Agencies

ONE of the most important, but least recognized, functions performed by organizations of the blindness system is to teach people who have difficulty seeing how to behave like blind people. This role-learning process has two stages. The first occurs as blind people are being screened into the blindness system, but before they become clients of agencies for the blind. The second occurs during the process of a client's rehabilitation. The purpose of this chapter is to analyze each of these two aspects of the socialization of the adult blind.

SOCIALIZATION DURING THE
RECRUITMENT PROCESS

The currently accepted administrative definition of blindness is used as the initial basis for determining who among the visually impaired are eligible to be recruited into the blindness system. By this definition, a person is blind if his corrected vision in the better eye does not exceed 10 percent of normal vision and/or if there is a specified delimitation of angular vision resulting from a defect in the visual field. Two points about this definition are important to recall. First, while a person who is qualified by it as blind has a very serious visual loss, he is by no means unable to see. With 10 percent, or even 5 percent, of normal vision, it is possible to function as a sighted person in most important areas of everyday life. Second, all but a tiny fraction of blind people in fact can see; the overwhelming majority of them have a measured visual acuity exactly at or very close to the line that demarcates the legally blind from those with severe visual impairment.

In order to determine whether persons with severely impaired vision are legally blind, it is necessary to give them a careful eye examination. This fact is one of the most important contingencies affecting their subsequent experiences. An unknown, but apparently substantial, portion of the legally blind population never comes to the attention of agencies for the blind because their visual acuity has never been tested. Research by Josephson suggests that many of these people subjectively experience their visual impairment as "trouble seeing"; neither they nor laymen who know them define their impairment as blindness.[1]

Others, however, experience their impairment as blindness. Their ability to perform ordinary domestic and job tasks may be significantly decreased; they may find it difficult or even impossible to read or watch television. Mobility may become a serious problem for them. The frustrations that sometimes result from visual loss may convince such a person that he is becoming blind and that he might benefit from the services and assistance offered by agencies and rehabilitation centers for the blind. Such a person often voluntarily presents himself to a local blindness agency for help. When this occurs he is given an eye examination in order to be certain that his visual acuity level falls within the currently accepted administrative definition of blindness.

Even those whose blindness has definitely been diagnosed by

[1] Eric Josephson, *The Social Life of Blind People*, Research Series No. 19, American Foundation for the Blind, New York, 1968.

medical authorities may nevertheless avoid agencies for the blind. The patient may ask his ophthalmologist not to report his name to a blindness register, or he may simply refuse the assistance offered him through the commission for the blind in his state. Among such individuals, self-definition of their visual impairment emphasizes the maximizing of remaining sight. They do not, therefore, regard agencies for the blind or rehabilitation centers as providing services relevant to their problems. Such persons usually seek vision-enhancement services from ophthalmologists, optometrists, and other eye specialists.

Not all people who have been labeled "blind" can follow a course entirely of their own choosing. Strong pressures are often exerted upon them to begin to think of themselves as blind. These pressures sometimes take the form of admonitions from others to "face the facts." More often, however, they are insidious, resulting subtly from the reactions of medical and welfare specialists, friends, family members, and even the impaired person himself to the new label that has been applied to him. Blindness has traditionally implied a complete absence of vision, a deficiency which, except for a miracle, is assumed to be incurable. Many ophthalmologists, physicians, workers for the blind, and laymen continue to respond to the word in this traditional sense. There is a tendency to treat the person who is blind by definition as though he has, or shortly will have, no vision at all, as though his condition is incurable and unimprovable. Once an ophthalmologist has determined that an individual is officially blind, he often refers the patient to a welfare authority with the reminder to "come back in a year for a check-up." This invitation implies that the ophthalmologist can do no more for the person because his problems are no longer medical ones of vision but psychological and social problems of adjustment to blindness.

The response of ophthalmologists to blindness is subjectively experienced by the person who is legally blind as an abrupt redefinition of his problem. Whereas he was previously treated as a sighted person who had difficulty seeing, he is now treated as a blind person who has residual vision. This fundamental redefinition is further reinforced when the blind person becomes a client in an agency for the blind. In such agencies, many of the basic techniques that were originally devised for persons who are completely blind may be taught to the blind person who has vision. Such persons may be expected to learn braille, even though special lenses would enable them to read ordinary or enlarged ink print. Often they are given the same training in the use of mechanical aids for mobility as totally blind persons, even though mobility may be perfectly possible with special lenses. They may also be trained for jobs that were originally devised for totally blind persons, even though remaining vision would enable them to continue doing the jobs they have always done. In these and other ways, the person whose vision is severely impaired is treated as if he were totally blind.

The impaired person is thus under strong pressure to think of himself as blind and to redefine his visual impairment from a medical problem of attenuated vision to a kind of welfare problem requiring extensive social services. Accompanying this phenomenon is a strong emphasis on psychological adjustment to blindness and personal acceptance of this condition. The visually impaired person's readiness for the offered services is measured by his willingness to admit to himself the fact of his blindness and to show that he is resigned to the alleged permanence of his condition.

Thus, when an individual's vision is slightly better than 10 percent of normal, he is regarded as a sighted person who has a severe visual loss. When his visual acuity drops below this arbitrary line, agents of the society begin to treat him as a blind person who possesses residual vision. While his vision exceeds the minimum level specified by the official definition, his seeing problem is treated as the legitimate concern of medicine. When he becomes officially blind, his condition is transformed into a social welfare problem. He is able and encouraged to function as a sighted person so long as his vision remains better than 20/200, but he is considered maladjusted if he continues to function this way when his vision drops below this line. The application of the label "blind" to individuals who can see therefore has enormous consequences in the way they are treated by specialists, family members, and friends.

Withstanding the force of these pressures is not easy. As a rule, there is a firm consensus encouraging the blind person to accept the official view of his condition. At the same time, the person usually experiences deep-seated fears about his visual impairment, which in-terfere with his ability to withstand the pressures on him. As a result, many persons who are officially blind succumb to the effects of label-ing and regard their condition as a social-service, rather than a medical, problem.

Some legally blind persons, of course, respond in other ways. Some refuse to admit any visual loss at all. This mechanism of de-nial inures them to the attitudes and responses of medical and wel-fare authorities to their condition. Others who recognize and fear the loss of vision live with the hope that their next annual visit to the ophthalmologist will produce some magic cure for their condi-tion. Others recognize the severity of their visual loss and deliber-ately set out to solve the mechanical, social, and psychological prob-lems that are occasioned by it. This requires an ability to master relevant social resources, an ability reserved for only a small seg-ment of any population in a society. As a result, many of the people who have been detected as blind according to the currently accepted administrative definition have no choice but to stay within the blind-ness system.

After blindness has been determined, the appropriate organiza-tions from which to seek assistance must be identified and evaluated. Where a blind person turns for help depends on the general informa-tion he has about the agencies for the blind. I refer here not only to knowledge of their existence, but also to beliefs and impressions about the kind and quality of services these agencies offer. Appar-ently, a whole set of beliefs about organizations for the blind are shared by people from all walks of life. For example, it is widely held that agencies for the blind are the legitimate and proper agents for the care of the blind. They are said to be staffed with highly quali-fied, well-trained experts who possess special knowledge about, and insight into, the complex and puzzling problems of the blind. Most laymen feel that it is natural and proper for a blind person to turn for help to an agency for the blind. These views create in the newly blinded person a positive psychological set, a readiness to accept workers for the blind as the persons best qualified to help him. Al-though disillusionment and doubt may later set in, during the earli-est phases of his socialization into the role of client, while he is most vulnerable to the beliefs, ideas, and advice of others, the average client accepts workers for the blind as *the* experts who will solve his problem. For a majority of blind persons, this acceptance is reinforced by the fact that there are no alternatives to these agencies in the community.

There are blind persons who have attempted to get help with their problems from individuals and organizations in the general service community. Some have gone to ministers, psychologists, psychiatrists, or social caseworkers for counseling. Some have gone to family service agencies for help with marital and other family problems. Others have approached local Y's in order to join in the recreation programs they sponsor. It is the common experience of most of these blind persons that the persons and organizations in the general community to whom they go for help refer them to the local agency for the blind. There are some cases, of course, in which such a referral is appropriate, since the person's problems are directly related to his blindness. But, in other instances, the blind person's problems are of the sort that unspecialized people or organizations are particularly suited to deal with. A family crisis precipitated by the onset of blindness in one of its members is a family problem and not a problem generic to blindness. The psychiatric problems experienced by some blind persons are similar to the psychiatric problems of many sighted persons. Because they are blind, however, these persons are referred to agencies for the blind by those to whom they go for assistance. The inflated beliefs about these agencies often stem from an unacknowledged desire on the part of the public to avoid contact with blind persons. This disguised message reinforces the blind person's eventual dependence on these agencies.

SOCIALIZATION WITHIN AGENCIES FOR THE BLIND

When a blind person first comes to an organization for the blind, he usually has some specific ideas about what his primary problems are and how they can be solved. Most new clients request services that they feel will solve or ameliorate the specific problems they experience because of their visual impairment. Many want only to be able to read better, and therefore request optical aids. Others desire help with mobility problems, or with special problems of dressing, eating, or housekeeping. Some need money or medical care. A few contact agencies for the blind in search of scientific discoveries that will restore their vision. Although the exact type of help sought varies considerably, many clients feel that the substance of their problems is contained in their specific requests. The few exceptions to this pattern are, by and large, the blind people who have been most completely victimized by the labeling process, who believe that all blind persons come to the agencies for help, and who have no concrete ideas about their problems.

The personal conceptions that blinded persons have about the nature of their problems are in sharp contrast with beliefs that workers for the blind share about the problems of blindness. The latter regard blindness as one of the most severe of all handicaps, the effects of which are long-lasting, pervasive, and extremely difficult to ameliorate. They believe that if these problems are to be solved, blind persons must understand them and all their manifestations and willingly submit themselves to a prolonged, intensive, and comprehensive program of psychological and restorative services. Effective socialization of the client largely depends upon changing his views about his problem. In order to do this, the client's views about the problems of blindness must be discredited. Workers must convince him that simplistic ideas about solving the problems of blindness by means of one or a few services are unrealistic. Workers regard the client's initial definition of his problems as akin to the visible portion of an iceberg. Beneath the surface of awareness lies a tremendously complicated mass of problems that must be dealt with before the surface problems can ever be successfully solved.

Discrediting the client's personal ideas about his problems is achieved in several ways. His initial statements about why he has come to the organization and what he hopes to receive from it are euphemistically termed "the presenting problem," a phrase that implies superficiality in the client's views. During the intake interview and then later with the caseworker or psychologist, the client is encouraged to discuss his feelings and aspirations. Workers regard this encouragement as necessary for a ventilation of the frustrations and confusion the client must inevitably feel. He is listened to attentively and sympathetically. However, when concrete plans are formulated, the client learns that his personal views about his problems are largely ignored. A client's request for help with a reading problem produces a recommendation by the worker for a comprehensive psychological work-up. A client's inquiries regarding the availability of financial or medical aid may elicit the suggestion that he enroll in a complicated long-term program of testing, evaluation, and training. In short, blind persons who are acceptable to the agency for the blind will often find that intake workers listen attentively to their views but then dismiss them as superficial or inaccurate.

Some clients voluntarily leave the agency either because they do not believe they are any less competent to judge their problems than a worker for the blind or because they have neither the time nor the inclination to subject themselves to a long-term program of restorative and evaluative services in order to acquire what they regard as simple skills. Other clients leave because they have problems the agency is unable to deal with. This is particularly true of the elderly, the multiply handicapped, and the uneducable or unemployable. For most persons who have come this far in the process, however, dropping out is not a particularly realistic alternative, since it implies that the blind person has other resources open to him. For the most part, such resources are not available.

I have implied that the experiences a blind person has before being inducted into an agency make him vulnerable to the wishes and intentions of the workers who deal with him. The ability to withstand the pressure to act, think, and feel in conformity with the workers' concept of a model blind person is further reduced by the fact that the workers have a virtual monopoly on the rewards and punishments in the system. By manipulating these rewards and punishments, workers are able to pressure the client into rejecting personal conceptions of problems in favor of the worker's own definition of them. Much evaluative work, in fact, involves attempts to get the client to understand and accept the agency's conception of the prob-

lems of blindness. This evaluation is usually done by trained psychologists, social caseworkers, and others who adopt the therapeutic
approach of the clinician. In face-to-face situations, the blind person is rewarded for showing insight and subtly reprimanded for
continuing to adhere to earlier notions about his problems. He is led
to think that he "really" understands past and present experiences
when he couches them in terms acceptable to his therapist. If he
persists in viewing his "presenting problems" as the real ones, he
is labeled "unacceptable" or "uninsightful." The client is said to be
"blocking," or resisting the truth. The psychological impact of this
treatment is, of course, very great. The willingness of the therapist
to accept a client is a potent force for people who are facing a severe crisis.

Psychological rewards are not the only rewards at stake in this
process. A fundamental tenet of work for the blind is that a client
must accept the fact of his blindness and everything implied by it
before he can be effectively rehabilitated. As a result, a client must
show signs of understanding his problem in the therapist's terms
before he will be permitted to progress any further in the program.
Since most blind persons are anxious to move along in the program
as rapidly as possible, the implications of being labeled "uncooperative" are serious. Such a label prevents him from receiving basic
restorative services. The uncooperative client is assigned low priority
for entering preferred job programs. Workers for the blind are less
willing to extend themselves on his behalf. As a result, the alert
client quickly learns to become "insightful," to behave as workers
expect him to.

Under these circumstances, the assumptions and theories of
workers for the blind concerning blindness and rehabilitation take
on new signficance, for what they do is to create, shape, and mold
the attitudes and behavior of the client in his role as a blind person.
In certain agencies, these attitudes and actions are taught to clients
in a deliberate, explicit fashion; in others, clients learn them by
drawing inferences about themselves from the attitudes of workers
toward them. In either case, it is in organizations for the blind that
theories and explicit and implicit assumptions about blindness and

rehabilitation become actualized in the clients' attitudes and behavior. We can therefore gain an understanding about the behavior of clients as blind people by examining the theories and assumptions about blindness and rehabilitation held by workers for the blind.

THE PRACTICE THEORIES OF BLINDNESS WORKERS

The beliefs, ideologies, and assumptions about blindness and rehabilitation that make up practice theories of work for the blind are legion. They include global and limited theories about blindness, ethical principles, commonsense ideas, and an array of specific beliefs that are unrelated, and often contradictory, to one another. Contained in this total array of ideas are two basically different approaches to the problems of blindness. The first I will call the "restorative approach"; the most complete and explicit version of this approach is contained in the writings of Father Thomas Carroll.[2] The second I will call the "accommodative approach." This approach has never been formulated into a codified practice theory; rather, it is only apparent in the programs and policies of more orthodox agencies for the blind.

The Restorative Approach

The basic premise of the restorative approach to blindness is that most blind people can be restored to a high level of independence enabling them to lead a reasonably normal life. However, these goals are attainable only if the person accepts completely the fact that he is blind, and only after he has received competent professional counseling and training.

Father Carroll's theory, which I will treat as a prototype of this approach, attempts to analyze the nature of blindness, what it does to ordinary people who are struck by it during their adult years, and

[2] Thomas J. Carroll, *Blindness: What It Is, What It Does, and How to Live with It*, Little, Brown & Company, Boston, 1961.

what can be done about it. According to Father Carroll, the loss of sight is a dying. "It is death," he writes, "to a way of life that had become part of the man. It is a destructive blow to the self-image which a man has carefully, though unconsciously, constructed throughout his lifetime, a blow almost to his being itself."[3] Those who become blind have a two-stage reaction. The first stage is shock, characterized by an inability to function or even to comprehend what has happened. The second stage is grief or bereavement, a kind of period of mourning for the life that is gone, the lost self. Father Carroll believes that a blind person must undergo the experiences of these two stages before he can be rehabilitated. He asserts, "Practically every patient must touch bottom before he begins the long road up."[4] This "long road up" is a new life for the blind person. Father Carroll believes that when the sighted person is "dead," "the blind person can once again become the same person, but only if he is willing to go through the pain of death to sight."[5]

The dying of which Father Carroll speaks consists of a series of losses forced on the blind person by his disability. These many losses interlock with one another, and are experienced simultaneously by the recently blinded person. "Each loss," writes Father Carroll, "involves a painful farewell (a death). But with the death of the sighted man, the blind man will be born. And the life that is his can be good."[6]

Seven basic kinds of losses resulting from blindness are identified: (1) the losses to psychological security—the losses of physical integrity, confidence in the remaining senses, reality contact with the environment, visual background, and light security; (2) the losses of the skills of mobility and techniques of daily living; (3) the communication losses, such as the loss of ease of written and spoken communication, and of information about daily events in the world; (4) the losses of appreciation, which include the loss of the visual perception of the pleasurable and of the beautiful; (5)

[3] *Ibid.*, p. 11.
[4] *Ibid.*, p. 12.
[5] *Ibid.*, pp. 12–13.
[6] *Ibid.*, p. 13.

the losses of occupational and financial status, which consist of financial security, career, vocational goals, job opportunities, and ordinary recreational activities; (6) the resulting losses to the whole personality, including the loss of personal independence, social adequacy, self-esteem, and total personality organization; and (7) the concomitant losses of sleep, of physical tone of the body, and of decision, and the sense of control over one's life.[7]

Rehabilitation, in this scheme, is the process "whereby adults in varying stages of helplessness, emotional disturbance, and dependence come to gain new understanding of themselves and their handicap, the new skills necessary for their state, and a new control of their emotions and their environment."[8] This process is not a simple one; it involves the pain and recurrent crises that accompany the acceptance of the many "deaths" to sighted life. It consists of "restorations" for each of the losses involved in blindness. The final objective of total rehabilitation involves returning and integrating the blinded person in his society.

This rehabilitation process logically divides into four main phases: training the other senses to take over the role of sight; training in basic skills and the use of various mechanical devices; restoring the sense of psychological security; and assisting the individual to meet the prevailing attitudes of the society toward him.[9] The various restorations in each of these phases correspond to the losses the person has encountered. The loss of confidence in the remaining senses is restored through deliberate training of these senses; the loss of mobility is restored through training in the use of a long cane or a guide dog; the loss of ease of written communication is restored through learning braille; and so on. The goal of this process is to reintegrate the components of the restored personality into an effectively functioning whole.

The philosophy expressed in Father Carroll's writings has been adopted in toto in several rehabilitation centers and general agencies

[7] *Ibid.,* pp. 14–79.
[8] *Ibid.,* p. 96.
[9] *Ibid.,* pp. 123–239.

for the blind in this country. In these organizations, the ideas contained in his book are used as the basis for a formal course taught to blind people while they are obtaining services. The purpose of this course is to clarify for them what they have lost because they are blind, how they must change through the course of rehabilitation, and what their lives will be like when rehabilitation has been completed. These ideas are given added weight by the fact that they are shared by all staff members who deal directly with the client and, in some agencies at least, by other nonservice personnel who have occasional contacts with clients.

Other organizations have borrowed only certain parts of Father Carroll's theory. As a rule, such agencies reject his notions of death and rebirth, substituting basic concepts of psychiatry and clinical psychology that relate to life crises and adjustment. The portions of Father Carroll's theory that are accepted by such agencies relate to his ideas about basic losses and restorations.

We cannot assume that there is a necessary correspondence between these beliefs regarding the limits and potentialities imposed by blindness and the blind client's self-image. The question of the full impact of the former on the latter is an empirical one on which there are no hard data. Our analysis of the client's "set" when he enters an agency for the blind does suggest, however, that such beliefs probably have a profound impact on his self-image. As I noted, when the client comes to an agency, he is often seeking direction and guidance and, more often than not, he is in a state of crisis. Consequently, the authority of the system makes the client highly suggestible to the attitudes of those whose help he seeks.

There is evidence that some blind people resist the pressures of the environment of agencies and centers that adopt this philosophy by feigning belief in the workers' ideas for the sake of "making out" in the system.[10] In such cases, the impact of workers on the client's self-image will be attenuated. Despite this, he will learn only those skills made available to him by the agency or center. These skills,

[10] *Information Bulletin No. 59*, University of Utah, Regional Rehabilitation Research Institute, Salt Lake City, 1968.

which the workers regard as opportunities for individual fulfillment, act also as limits. The choice of compensatory skills around which the theory revolves means the exclusion of a spectrum of other possibilities.

The Accommodative Approach

A basic premise of the restorative approach is that most blind people possess the capacity to function independently enough to lead normal lives. Rehabilitation centers and general service agencies that have embraced this approach therefore gear their entire service programs toward achieving this goal. In other agencies for the blind, no disagreement is voiced about the desirability of blind peoples' attaining independence, but there is considerable skepticism as to whether this is a feasible goal for more than a small fraction of the client population.[11] According to this view, blindness poses enormous obstacles to independence—obstacles seen as insurmountable by a majority of people. Occasionally, a few highly gifted blind people, through great personal effort, are able to achieve independence. Such persons are regarded as "amazing," as rare utopian models of the highest ideals of workers for the blind. To gear programs to such persons would be a serious error, however, since the bulk of clients cannot benefit from them. A different approach, which I will call "accommodative," is required for such clients. Settings and programs are designed to accommodate the helpless, dependent blind person.

The physical environment in such agencies is often contrived specifically to suit certain limitations inherent in blindness. In some agencies, for example, the elevators have tape recorders that report the floor at which the elevator is stopping and the direction in which it is going, and panels of braille numbers for each floor as well. Other agencies have mounted over their front doors special bells that ring at regular intervals to indicate to blind people that they

[11] Roger G. Barker *et al.*, *Adjustment to Physical Handicap and Illness: A Survey of the Social Psychology of Physique and Disability*, Social Science Research Council, New York, 1953.

are approaching the building. Many agencies maintain fleets of cars to pick up clients at their homes and bring them to the agency for services. In the cafeterias of many agencies, special precautions are taken to serve only food that blind people can eat without awkwardness. In one agency cafeteria, for example, the food is cut before it is served, and only spoons are provided.

Recreation programs in agencies that have adopted the accommodative approach consist of games and activities tailored to the disability. For example, bingo, a common activity in many programs, is played with the aid of a corps of volunteers who oversee the game, attending to anything the blind person is unable to do himself.

Employment training for clients in accommodative agencies involves instruction in the use of equipment specifically adapted to the disability. Work tasks, and even the entire method of production, are engineered with this disability in mind, so that there is little resemblance between an average commercial industrial setting and a sheltered workshop. Indeed, the blind person who has been taught to do industrial work in a training facility of an agency for the blind will acquire skills and methods of production that may be unknown in most commercial industries.

The general environment of such agencies is also accommodative in character. Clients are rewarded for trivial things and praised for performing tasks in a mediocre fashion. This superficial and overgenerous reward system makes it impossible for most clients to assess their accomplishments accurately. Eventually, since anything they do is praised as outstanding, many of them come to believe that the underlying assumption must be that blindness makes them incompetent.

The unstated assumption of accommodative agencies is that most of their clients will end up organizing their lives around the agency. Most will become regular participants in the agency's recreation programs, and those who can work will obtain employment in a sheltered workshop or other agency-sponsored employment program. The accommodative approach therefore produces a blind person who can function effectively only within the confines of the

agency's contrived environment. He learns skills and behavior that
are necessary for participating in activities and programs of the
agency, but which make it more difficult to cope with the environment of the larger community. A blind person who has been fully
socialized in an accommodative agency will be maladjusted to the
larger community. In most cases, he does not have the resources, the
skills, the means, or the opportunity to overcome the maladaptive
patterns of behavior he has learned. He has little choice but to remain a part of the environment that has been designed and engineered to accommodate him.

This portrayal of accommodative agencies suggests that the workers in them, like those in restorative agencies, make certain assumptions about the limitations that blindness imposes, and that these
assumptions are manifested in expectations about attitudes and behavior that people ought to have because they are blind. The differ-
ing expectations of accommodative and restorative agencies is suggested by the nomenclature for the blind person in each kind of
agency. Restorative agencies call those they serve "trainees"; accommodative agencies use the term "client." "Trainee" is a temporary
status, suggesting that a person is being prepared for some future
and different status, that learning is occurring, and that an element
of personal autonomy exists and is being exercised. The term "client"
refers to someone who is under the protection or patronage of another, a dependent. It suggests that the person is capable of doing
little, and that he should passively accept what is given to him by
his patrons. This term also has a ring of permanency to it, suggesting that little can be done to change his plight.

Unfortunately, no hard data are available on socialization outcomes in agencies that adopt either of the two approaches I have
described. However, the materials I collected from interviews with
blind people suggest that a number of discernably patterned reactions occur.[12] Some clients and trainees behave according to work-

[12] Most of this discussion applies to blind people who have been exposed
to agencies that adopt an accommodative approach to rehabilitation. Little
information could be gathered on those who have been trainees in restorative agencies, primarily because such agencies are comparatively few in
number and recent in origin.

ers' expectations of them deliberately and consciously in order to extract from the system whatever rewards it may have. Others behave according to expectations because they have accepted and internalized them as genuine qualities of character. The former are the "expedient" blind people, and the latter are the "true believers."

Expedient blind people consciously play a part, acting convincingly the way they sense their counselors and instructors want them to act. They develop a keen sense of timing that enables them to be at their best when circumstances call for it. When the circumstances change, the facade is discarded, much as the Negro discards his "Uncle Tomisms" in the absence of whites. As a rule, the expedient blind person is one who recognizes that few alternatives are open to him in the community; his response is an understandable effort to maximize his gains in a bad situation.

True believers are blind people for whom workers' beliefs and assumptions about blindness are unquestioned ideals toward which they feel impelled earnestly to strive. While this pattern is probably found in all agencies for the blind, it is most obvious in those which embrace the accommodative approach to blindness. Clients who become true believers in such agencies actually experience the emotions that workers believe they must feel. They experience and spontaneously verbalize the proper degree of gratitude, they genuinely believe themselves to be helpless, and they feel that their world must be one of darkness and dependency. Although, in all likelihood, only a minority of all clients and trainees conform to this pattern, they are highly visible because they embody many of the qualities of the blindness stereotype, and are so frequently displayed to the public by agencies, both as a justification for their existence and as evidence of their good works.

A third type of socialization outcome, the "professional" blind, are persons whose lives are almost entirely organized within some part of the blindness system. They may be unemployed blind people who spend most of their time in agencies for the blind, where they seek recreation, counseling, and companionship. These people have few contacts with the wider community; if they are not at the agency, they are usually at home. Any contacts with the larger community that do occur—such as visits to the doctor or dentist, shopping, or filing income tax returns—are usually mediated through the agency of which they are a client.

Another kind of professional blind person is the client who, in the course of his rehabilitation, acquires the expertise to fill a position in a sheltered workshop or other agency-sponsored program, or in special direct-service activities within the blindness agency itself. Such jobs include working in sheltered workshops, running vending stands, repairing talking-book machines, running braille presses, working as home teachers, assisting in craftshop and workshop programs, working in piano-tuning or music schools, or doing preliminary screening and counseling of clients. Almost none of these people have high job aspirations. Most are hired because of the agency's good will; if it were to close its doors or dismiss them for any reason, they would probably have a difficult time securing other jobs. Thus there is a high degree of commitment on the part of such blind people to the agencies for which they work.

Finally, among the professional blind are those who have had some professional training. Many of them have been blind from a very young age and have grown up in the blindness system. Some are graduates of residential schools; others have been clients of agencies for the blind from earliest childhood. These persons often select work for the blind as a career. Many do so out of a genuine concern for the plight of the blind, whom they desire to help, and others are motivated by the recognition that it would be difficult and even impossible for them to secure employment elsewhere.[13] Some of these people feel a strong commitment to the status quo; others deliberately enter this field in order to change it. They help to counterbalance the highly conservative elements in the field.

One other pattern can be discerned among clients and trainees of agencies for the blind—the independent blind person. It consists of those blind people who return to their original jobs or secure other competitive employment. Many rejoin their original circle of friends

---

[13] *Home Teachers of the Adult Blind: What They Do; What They Could Do; What Will Enable Them to Do It*, American Association of Workers for the Blind, Inc., Washington, D.C., 1961.

or otherwise assume roles in the community that they once played. These are the blind people who attempt to lead average, normal lives within the constraints imposed upon them by their handicap. Statistically, this group is probably the smallest of all the subgroups of the blindness population. In order for a blind person to become independent, he must usually possess substantial personal resources, supportive and understanding friends, and an unusual ability, talent, or quality that overrides the stigmatizing effects of his handicap. Personal wealth or even a moderate independent income may enable the blind person to purchase part of his independence. His success also depends upon the willingness of family members, friends and close associates to permit him to make the adjustments necessary for independence.

This, then, is the nature of the socialization of the blind within the blindness system. We can conclude from this analysis that the ways in which individual blind people experience their condition and the general problems and behavior patterns of blind people are profoundly affected by the organized intervention programs of the blindness system. It is clear that the very nature of the phenomenon of blindness is as much a product of these social forces as it is of any other types of forces that can be identified.

CHAPTER 6

Determinants of a Blindness

Agency's Approach

to Rehabilitation

A CURIOUS fact about the blindness system in America is that while almost all organizations of the blind uphold the desirability of a restorative approach to rehabilitation, most of them follow an accommodative approach in practice. One reason for this paradox is that an agency's practices reflect not only the beliefs and values of its staff but its responses to certain economic, manpower, and community pressures as well. Three such pressures are especially important in this regard: relationships between blindness organizations and the communities that support them; relationships among blindness organizations situated in the same communities; and certain features of the recruitment, selection, and retention of personnel for agencies for the blind. Each of these factors affects the approach toward rehabilitation assumed by a particular blindness agency.

BLINDNESS AGENCIES AND THE COMMUNITY

Relationships between blindness agencies and the community are extremely superficial. Such organizations are socially isolated even though most of them are situated in the heart of a busy urban area. By and large, the only persons who enter or leave the organization's premises are those who are employed or served by it. Few laymen have ever visited an agency for the blind, and fewer still are familiar with its programs and activities. Occasions when blind clients enter the community are also rare. Most of their day is spent in the agency or at home. Workers for the blind and clients therefore occupy isolated islands in the midst of areas that provide the best conditions for contact and interaction with the community at large.

This paradox is heightened by two additional facts. Most blindness organizations receive liberal financial support from the community. In New York City alone, I have estimated that the yield of direct appeals to the public by private agencies for the blind is about $20,000,000, and the solvency of only a few blindness organizations in the entire country is genuinely in doubt. Furthermore, most laymen have a very favorable impression of agencies for the blind even though few of them have ever had the kind of exposure to blindness organizations that would enable them to make intelligent judgments about the quality and effectiveness of their work. As a rule, the mere mention of an organization for the blind is enough to call forth expressions of praise and admiration.

The superficiality of agency-community relationships is also reflected in the quality of official contacts between blind clients and the community. Such contacts are both rare and highly contrived. Clients are carefully selected, the encounters are short, and the social roles played by participants are highly stereotyped. A distinctive emotional climate pervades these meetings, consisting of a subtle blend of pathos, amiability, gratitude, wonder, praise, humor, and tension. Typically, blind clients make a statement concerning their plight before coming to an agency for help, the kinds of help they have received, the changes the agency has brought about in their lives, the happiness that is now theirs, and the gratitude they feel toward the agency and its benefactors. Such testimonials comprise a major part of the contact that occurs between blind clients and the community.

This superficiality is the logical outcome of a number of deep-seated and often unrecognized feelings held by many sighted people about blindness. As suggested in Chapter 2, these feelings are the product of four forces: stereotypic beliefs about the nature of this handicap, its causes, and its consequences for feelings, mood states, and behavior; the fact that this condition is a stigma viewed by the sighted with intense fear and dread; the normative ambiguities and behavioral uncertainties that inevitably arise in encounters between blind and sighted people; and, finally, the socially dependent relationship of blind people to the seeing. These combined forces lead many sighted people to avoid social interaction with the blind.

This disposition toward avoidance has far-reaching implications for the functions thrust upon blindness agencies by the community that supports them. For one thing, such agencies are prone to become asylums for this segment of the unwanted of the community.[1] Blind people are strongly encouraged to seek assistance at blindness agencies, but there is covert, yet stubborn, resistance in the community to any genuine movement of blind people from the agency back into the mainstream of community life. In fact, the blind person who deliberately thrusts himself into the everyday life of the community is soon treated as a nuisance, and the blindness worker who pursues too seriously the avowed goal of reintegration soon wears out his welcome in the community. Moreover, the agency for the blind that genuinely stresses the reintegration of its clients may have difficulty raising enough money to keep its doors open. This sequestering of the blind from the community not only minimizes the occasions for contact between the sighted and the blind, but also decreases the visibility of the problem. The blindness agency that is able to contain blind people and to control their access to the community decreases awareness of the problem within the community.

An accommodative approach to rehabilitation can be viewed as one type of response to the pressures arising from community re-

---

[1] Erving Goffman, *Asylums*, Doubleday & Company, Inc., New York, 1961.

actions to blindness. Basic assertions made about the blind by advocates of the accommodative approach—that most blind people are incapable of true independence, or that most of them prefer their own company, or that the blind need to perform certain special kinds of work because of their disability—are an ideological justification for an agency's treatment of blind clients in a manner more compatible with the needs of the larger community than with those of blind people. The needs of the blind are not determined from scientific studies of the impact of blindness on the functioning of the human organism; they are invented to justify the creation of the programs and institutional arrangements required to palliate community reactions and fears about blindness.

Among the many reasons some blindness agencies are so sensitive to community fears and reactions, undoubtedly the single most important one is that they are heavily dependent upon the community for financial support. Historically, it seems to be the case that the blindness agencies sponsoring programs compatible with the community need to minimize awareness of the blind have had the most success in raising funds for their operations, while the agencies adopting a restorative approach to rehabilitation have experienced the most serious financial problems. This lesson of history in the blindness field has not been forgotten; indeed, it has probably been overlearned.

The sequestering of blind people from the community by blindness agencies is not accomplished without certain psychological costs both to the community and to workers in the agencies. A deep-seated, abiding sense of guilt often develops in both groups, stemming from the recurring suspicion that blind people (or any other unwanted groups, for that matter) may not always find the arrangements provided for them compatible with their needs and aspirations. There is a gnawing doubt in the minds of many that the blind may not desire only the company of others who are blind; that they may not have entirely lost a desire or ability to be independent; or that they may continue to desire the freedom to make vital decisions affecting their own lives. The sense of guilt accompanying the institutional arrangements of the accommodative approach to rehabilitation therefore threatens the self-esteem of the sighted and of blindness workers. Both groups need and continually seek assurances that blind people actually prefer these institutional arrangements over any others that could be established. As a result, the role of client in many accommodative agencies involves continual expressions of gratitude toward his benefactors and contentment with his lot.

It is clear that a blindness agency has not one, but two, audiences —blind people and the community in which the organization is located. An agency's relationships with its second audience determine the nature of its relationships to the first. The substance of these relationships and their impact on the socialization of clients are nowhere more apparent than in the varied and frequent fundraising activities of private accommodative agencies for the blind. The agency sponsors regular social benefits to which it invites the wealthy elite of the community. At periodic dinners the agency honors celebrities from the entertainment or sports world. Acting companies, symphonic groups, and individual entertainers hold benefit performances. Finally, direct appeals to the larger public are conducted through the mails and by means of canisters in stores and shops in the community.

Fund-raising activities that involve direct encounters with laymen follow a typical pattern. Initially, a lucid portrayal is given of the plight of the blind in society. The potential benefactors are poignantly reminded of how unfortunate are those who cannot see. Graphic descriptions are given of the effects blindness can have on such matter-of-fact activities as eating, walking, reading, dressing, and conversing with others in routine social situations. Often, blind clients are called upon to describe the deep despair they felt when their vision failed them, and the tragic consequences of their blindness. These portrayals emphasize that most sighted persons cannot or do not appreciate how lucky they are that their vision is intact. The audience is reminded that no one can ever be completely immunized against becoming blind. Many of the case histories are of ordinary men and women who have suddenly lost their vision through accident or disease. Heavy emphasis is given to the part played by the sighted in contributing to the plight of the blind.

Through case histories and testimonials, the audience is informed about the extent of discrimination against the blind in areas of work, recreation, and general community life. These themes of the heavy burden that falls to the blind and of the ways in which the sighted unwittingly contribute to it arouse the audience's fears and latent guilt feelings about the blind.

The focus now changes from the blind person to the agency for the blind. Its history, contributions to the blind, prestige in the community and in the field of work for the blind, and current programs and plans are outlined. Clients are called upon to sing the agency's praises; to express gratitude for all it has done for them; and to assure those present that the blind prefer things as they are, that the solutions to the problems of blindness recommended by the agency are acceptable to them. This shift in emphasis identifies the organization as the legitimate and proper agent for solving the social problems of the blind. The need for expertise in dealing with the complicated problems of the blind and the importance of specialized programs and facilities are stressed. Most important, the audience is warned of the danger of leaving the education, rehabilitation, and retraining of the blind to naive, inexperienced people.

This information poses a dilemma for the audience. They have been told that persons like themselves contribute mightily to the problems of blind persons, that agencies and workers for the blind are best equipped and qualified to handle these complicated problems, and that laymen should not become directly involved in the helping process, since good intentions alone often do more harm than good. How then can the layman help? By what means can his guilt be alleviated?

A solution to the dilemma is proposed. The layman is told that the most important contribution he can make toward solving the problems of the blind is to provide funds to enable agencies and workers to apply their expertise. This suggestion provides the audience with a clear, important, and relatively painless part to play in helping the blind. By the act of donating money, the pent-up feelings of guilt aroused earlier can be discharged; it is understandable that so many sighted persons find the benefactor role palatable.

Many of the themes that run through these audience appeals are also found in the direct-mail and canister programs. The chief difference is that the sob-appeal element is much more intense and dramatic in mail and canister campaigns than in audience appeals. Posters, brochures, and other displays must catch the eye of the passer-by and of the average person who daily receives many pieces of junk mail. Consequently, fund raisers have traditionally employed pictures and themes that tap the deepest emotions of the largest number of people. Pictures are usually of healthy, attractive blind young people and adults, wearing expressions of pathos, gratitude, contentment, and hopefulness.

Fund-raising activities of both types are generally quite successful. At the same time, they have important implications for the functions that blindness agencies come to perform. For one thing, the benefactor role assigned the layman clearly implies that his principal, if not entire, obligation to blind people has been discharged by donating money. As a result, he is provided with a convenient excuse for refusing to cooperate with workers for the blind in areas that could make a crucial difference in terms of integrating the blind person into the community. When, for example, placement workers attempt to secure jobs for their clients in commercial industry, potential employers can politely and legitimately refuse them by pointing out that they have already discharged their responsibilities to the blind by making a generous donation to a blindness agency. This assertion is documented by publicly displaying the handsomely framed citation the agency gave the employer in recognition of his financial contribution.

Second, the success of many fund-raising campaigns by blindness agencies can be attributed to manipulation of the fears and erroneous beliefs the sighted have toward the blind. Blindness agencies may therefore develop a vested interest in preserving in sighted people the very attitudes and fears they assert are a major cause of the blind person's problems. A significant fact about the blindness system is that its public education function is largely defunct. With perhaps one or two exceptions, agencies for the blind do not sponsor programs genuinely intended to change society's reactions to the blind. Public education in most agencies means informing laymen about services the agencies provide their clients. It is likely that any broadening of such programs to include a direct assault on public fears and misconceptions would result in smaller contributions to many private blindness agencies.

Third, fund-raising campaigns inaccurately portray the true nature of the social and welfare problem of blindness in our society. As we have seen, the success of these campaigns depends upon strong emotional appeals. As a result, these campaigns exploit a number of cultural stereotypes in our society concerning blindness, youth, work, and hope. The agencies project an image of blind persons as either educable children or young, employable adults who can be helped to overcome a serious handicap and become materially productive. These appeals leave the unmistakable but erroneous impression that most blind people are young, educable, and employable. This view of the problem is highly acceptable to the public, since it masks distasteful truths about the real nature of the problem. The fact that the public has come to expect measurable results in terms of education and employment leads the agency to search for and retain clients who fit the public image of the blindness population and to reject blind persons who are multiply handicapped, unemployable, untrainable, and uneducable—in other words, the bulk of the blindness population.

The blindness agencies that employ these highly successful fund-raising techniques have very little choice but to adopt an accommodative approach to rehabilitation. Perhaps the most insidious consequence of the vicious cycle, beginning when an agency accedes to the avoidance reactions to blindness by laymen, is that the blind who have been victimized by this arrangement are ultimately required to give the public assurances that captivity is their genuine desire.

RELATIONSHIPS AMONG BLINDNESS AGENCIES IN THE SAME COMMUNITY

A second factor that has an important influence on an agency's approach to rehabilitation (particularly in agencies located in large metropolitan areas) is the nature of its relationships with other blindness agencies in the same community. My analysis of the "fit" between the needs of people in the blindness population and the services offered them by the blindness system suggests that there is a proliferation of services for a limited segment of the blind population. In view of the fact that there are only about one million blind people in the entire country, the number of visually impaired people living in any particular geographical area is usually quite small. There are probably only about 40,000 to 50,000 blind people in all of New York City, about 10,000 in Philadelphia, and about 15,000 in the Boston metropolitan area.[2] Yet there are more than 800 agencies and organizations for the blind in this country, a majority of which are situated in large urban areas. New York City has 50 separate organizations for the blind, 38 of which offer direct services;[3] Philadelphia has 14 major direct service agencies;[4] and the greater metropolitan area of Boston has 13 major agencies of this type.[5] Since a majority of these agencies offer services only to children and/or employable adults, there is a very high ratio of agencies to clients. In New York City, for example, 3 major and 6 smaller agencies offer direct social and educational services to an estimated 1,850 blind children living in the area. Even if we assume that none of these children is multiply handicapped, which we cannot, the agency-client ratio is very large indeed. Twenty-two organizations and agencies provide direct rehabilitation and vocational services to an estimated 12,000 blind persons who are of working age. This figure is somewhat inflated because between 50 and 60 percent of blind persons 18 to 54 years of age are women, for whom employment is not always a realistic or appropriate objective. Eleven other organizations specialize in the production and distribution of braille books and recordings for the blind. In addition, a number of state and federal services are available to the blind of New York City.

[2] These estimates were derived by computing the blindness rate per thousand of the population and adjusting the result to the population of each city.

[3] *Directory of Agencies Serving Blind Persons in the United States*, 15th ed., American Foundation for the Blind, New York, 1967, pp. 124–131.

[4] *Ibid.*, pp. 160–162.

[5] *Ibid.*, pp. 86–87.

The disproportionately large number of agencies offering services has many consequences for blind persons, for agencies for the blind, and for the community that supports them. One inevitable consequence is that competition for clients develops among agencies for the blind in the same metropolitan areas. The intensity of this competition varies, of course, with fluctuations in the availability of suitable clients. For example, when the Second World War erupted and jobs for blind persons in commercial industry became widely available, intense competition for clients developed.[6] By the same token, competition for blind children diminished somewhat when their numbers increased as a result of retrolental fibroplasia.[7] As these children became adults, the intensity of the competition increased.

In some instances, competition for clients has become so keen that it has been necessary for outside persons to intervene in order to keep the peace and to protect the welfare of those involved.[8] During periods of greatest competition, pirating of clients is not unknown, especially in urban areas that have not been previously designated as "the territory" of one or another agency.

The intense and sometimes ruthless competition between agencies for clients who fit their programs affects the agency's relationship to its clients. When an agency has the opportunity to provide services to a suitable blind person, it is reluctant to let him go completely. Finding a suitable replacement is always an uncertain matter, and without a substantial number of clients on hand, the agency may find it difficult to justify its expenditures to the public that supports it. Employment is secured for these persons in the agency's sheltered workshops, free recreational services are provided by the agency on an indefinite basis, and residential homes are sometimes maintained. Gradually, a greater and greater portion of the client's contact with the larger community is mediated by the agency, until the blind

[6] Hector Chevigny and Sydell Braverman, *The Adjustment of the Blind*, Yale University Press, New Haven, 1950.

[7] Retrolental fibroplasia is a disorder of the eye resulting from an excess of oxygen in the body. An epidemic of this disorder occurred in the 1940's and early 1950's among premature infants who had been placed in faulty incubators. Since these incubators were replaced, the disorder has virtually disappeared.

[8] Chevigny and Braverman, *op. cit.*, Chap. 12.

person is literally sequestered from the community. The accommodative approach to rehabilitation can be viewed as one kind of agency response to pressure from competitors. Clearly, this approach is compatible with the posture an agency may have to adopt with its clients in order to enhance its competitive position.

I have already suggested that one of the major reasons agencies compete for the young and the employable while the rest of the blindness population goes relatively unserved is that they fit the stereotype exploited in fund-raising campaigns relating blindness to youth, work, and hope. Another important reason for selectivity relates to the concepts that guided pioneers of work for the blind. Many of these concepts, formulated over a hundred years ago, make up a large part of contemporary theory in this field. They reflect the different demographic characteristics of the blind population at the inception of work for the blind. Since the number of persons in the general population who survived childhood and lived to old age was low, the number of elderly blind persons was also low. A major cause of blindness in the adult population at that time was industrial accidents. Ordinarily, the eyes were the only organs involved, so that these adult blind persons were healthy working people whose only handicap was blindness.[9] A substantial number of children were blinded at birth because of germs that specifically affected the eyes.[10] Because a majority of the blind in the late nineteenth century were children and adults of working age, the concepts in this field stressed education and employment. Through the years, these concepts have not changed in response to changing social, economic, and public health conditions. In addition, many workers for the blind have assumed that the problems of education and employment are inherent in the condition of blindness. They have mistaken these concepts for the problems of blindness itself. They view the blind to whom the concepts cannot easily be applied as marginal to the "real work" in services for the blind, which is educational and vocational. If a person cannot benefit from either of these services, his problems are de-

[9] Harry Best, *Blindness and the Blind in the United States,* The Macmillan Company, New York, 1934, Chap. 4.
[10] *Ibid.,* Chap. 3.

fined as insoluble and his case is closed. Elderly blind persons, the multiply handicapped, and the unemployable are considered apart from the "real problems" of blindness, because of these outdated concepts. Where commitment to these concepts diminishes, there has been a corresponding decline in the competition for clients.

THE SELECTION, RECRUITMENT, AND RETENTION OF WORKERS BY AGENCIES FOR THE BLIND

A final factor with important consequences for the kind of approach to rehabilitation an agency adopts is the method by which its professional staff is selected, recruited, and retained. One of the most important characteristics of blindness workers is that they are extremely heterogeneous with respect to education and social background. The present leaders in this field include people who hold the Ph.D. degree and people who have not graduated from high school; they include some who were born into the upper-middle and upper classes of our society and some who are from the working and lower classes. This social and educational heterogeneity suggests an extremely important fact about the nature of expertise in the field of work for the blind. Since many workers have had no formal training and there are few college-level programs in which training in this field can be obtained, expertise as a blindness worker is acquired almost entirely through work experience.

One consequence is that persons with little or no formal education can work themselves into positions of great influence and power in the field. To be sure, in almost all programs, the well-trained person receives priority over the one who has had no formal training at all, and there is every indication that it will become increasingly difficult to gain entree into work for the blind without at least some formal training. There are, however, a few enclaves in this field in which untrained persons who are ambitious can move into positions of substantial power and authority; and there are almost no programs that do not have at least some untrained workers who established themselves in influential positions before the dispute concern-

ing professionalizing the field developed. There is, therefore, a highly
vocal and influential group of workers for the blind whose claim to
technical competence rests entirely on their years of hard-earned experiences with blind persons. At the present time, these people are
probably a minority of all workers, but they control a disproportionately large number of key positions in the field. Some of them display
as much knowledge about, and sensitivity to, the problems of the
blind as the most highly trained professional workers in the field.
In fact, the content of at least some of the courses now offered in
graduate training programs for mobility instructors and rehabilitation counselors is based upon the advice and experience of these persons. They differ, however, from many professionally trained persons in at least one key respect: Their power and influence are tied
to the specific organization whose ranks they control, and their
status therefore depends heavily upon the continued functioning of
the agency with which they are identified. The professional worker
can leave one blindness agency for another or even leave the field
completely, since he is usually able to secure a job in the general
welfare field with roughly the same influence and opportunity. The
untrained worker, and especially the one who has had no formal
education, cannot do this. He often occupies a position which pays
him more than he could earn outside work for the blind, and which
gives him much greater authority, power, and prestige than his educational credentials would ordinarily merit. These benefits are usually specific to one agency for the blind. If such a person is director
of a major program in an agency and that agency closes its doors,
in all probability he will not be able to secure a comparable position
in another agency for the blind; and he most assuredly will not be
able to secure a comparable position outside the field of work for the
blind. The fate of the untrained worker is therefore directly tied up
with the fate of the agency for which he works. As a result, his primary commitment is to the agency. His commitment to work for the
blind as a profession and, more importantly, to the blind persons
who are served is only secondary.

Because of this, the ordinary worker for the blind is often forced
to opt for policies that ensure the continuation of his agency, even

when such policies may be detrimental to the welfare of the client. No such worker can afford to ignore the fact that an accommodative approach will ensure, and a restorative approach jeopardize, the fiscal integrity of his agency. Under these circumstances, it is not surprising that such workers cling tenaciously to the ideologies that justify an accommodative approach to rehabilitation.

This analysis suggests that the accommodative approach to rehabilitation contains many of the features of an ideology. This term, which is borrowed from studies of political conflict, implies that some of the beliefs that blindness workers hold about what blind people need or want are bound up with their vested interests and those of the agencies that employ them. "Needs" of blind people are shaped, molded, and even invented ex post facto to explain why service programs exist. These needs are not "discovered" by independent scientific inquiry; rather, they are the needs that blind people must have if they are to fit into and be served by programs that have arisen for other reasons. This point can be illustrated by a simple example. During the period of my field work for this study, I had an interview with the director of program services of a large multifunctional agency for the blind. When I inquired about the agency's practice theory, I was told that it was only recently that the question of the agency's philosophy had arisen. As this worker put it, "In the old days we knew what we were doing; it was only recently that we thought it would be a good idea to sit down and have our staff write out what we believe." Staff members submitted their statements of philosophy to this worker, who then put together a broad statement of the ideas that lay behind the agency's practices. The format of the statement was that blind people have needs A, B, and C and that, in recognition of these needs, this agency had established programs X, Y, and Z. As I leafed through the statement I came upon a pronouncement that the agency had always believed that people who have been recently blinded have a deep need to restore their confidence in themselves; and, in recognition of this fact, the agency had established a special program enabling them to do so. Penciled in on the side of the typewritten page was, "We don't believe this anymore." After investigating further, I learned that the benefactor of the program had withdrawn support for it. Since the program eliminated, it followed that the need that had justified it was also extinguished!

This inverted logic applies not only to public explanations of an organization's program; it may also be applied with equal force to the client. Over time, the belief often develops that a blind person must need what the agency offers; if the client fails to recognize this or does not wish to receive the offered service, it is felt that there is something wrong with him. In this sense, the cooperative client is the one who accepts the services offered; the uncooperative client is the one who fails to recognize in himself the needs to which agency programs correspond. It is easy to be deluded about the reality of these needs. There are always blind clients to whom blindness workers can turn for confirmation of these beliefs. These clients have been socialized, which is to say, trained to need and often depend upon the programs that are offered them. They are then used to confirm the fact that blind people have the needs the agency's philosophy says they have.

Essentially, then, the kind of approach adopted in the rehabilitation programs of a blindness agency is only partly a function of the beliefs and convictions of staff members; it also reflects the agency's responses to economic, political, and social forces in the community and in the profession of work for the blind.

CHAPTER 7

Living Without

Blindness Agencies

MY analysis of the selection process
used by blindness agencies indicates that many people who are blind
according to the currently accepted administrative definition of the
term have had little or no sustained contact with organizations for
the blind, and that at least some of those who have had contact
eventually come to live their lives outside the blindness system.
Those who have never been clients or trainees of blindness institutions can be divided into two subcategories: those who have never
been detected as blind by authorities in the blindness system and
those who are known to the blindness system but, for a variety of reasons, have never become clients or trainees in it. Those who have had
contact with blindness agencies can be grouped into three subcategories: those who have completed rehabilitation and vocational
training and are now living independently in their home communities; those who have deliberately disengaged themselves from blindness organizations in order to make a living by begging; and blinded

veterans of the armed forces of the United States, most of whom receive special rehabilitation, medical and financial benefits because of their blindness.

THE HIDDEN BLIND

The existence of legally blind people who are unknown to the blindness system is inferred from the major prevalence estimates of blindness. Even though their vision is severely impaired, many of these people have never gone to an ophthalmologist. Others, an unknown number, have had eye examinations that revealed visual acuity low enough to meet the level stipulated in the current definition of blindness but have apparently requested their physicians not to report this to the blindness register.

Because they are hidden, less is known about this group than any other in the blindness population. The only reliable data about the hidden blind come from a study by Josephson and Sussman of the prevalence of vision impairment in Cleveland.[1] These investigators set out to test the comparative cost and effectiveness of telephone sampling techniques with the traditional case-findings methods employed in most epidemiological studies. In the nearly 3,700 households they canvassed, these investigators were able to identify 50 percent more cases of blindness than were known to the local society for the blind through its blindness registers. A majority of the blind who were unknown in the blindness system were uneducated lower-class people. Since the only purpose of the study was to evaluate a method for obtaining data, little information was collected about the nature of the experiences of the hidden blind. The importance of such a study for evaluating the theory and practice of work for the blind certainly needs stressing.

THE UNSERVED DETECTED BLIND

Because they are somewhat visible, more is known about the unserved detected blind than about the hidden blind. The most reliable and valid data come from a study by Josephson of 684 people who

[1] Eric Josephson, and Marvin B. Sussman, "A Pilot Study of Visual Impairment," American Foundation for the Blind, New York, 1965, mimeographed.

were listed on blindness registers in four states.[2] The purposes of his study were to determine the needs of this population of blind people, how many of them were receiving services from local private and governmental agencies serving the blind, and what personal and social characteristics differentiated those who were receiving assistance from those who were not.

Josephson divided respondents in terms of the number of services they had ever received from agencies or organizations for the blind. For purposes of analysis, he compared those who had received no help from social agencies for the blind (whom he called "the unaided") with the aided. He found a number of important differences between the two groups: the unaided were older, were older when they lost their sight, had lower family income, were less educated, and were more isolated and less socially and culturally active than the blind receiving aid from blindness agencies.[3] Josephson asked the unaided group if they had any unmet needs. Eleven percent mentioned financial aid; 10 percent said they needed medical care; 8 percent mentioned a need for help with travel; and another 7 percent expressed a desire for vocational training.[4]

These data indicate that the unserved detected blind probably include large numbers of poor, uneducated, elderly people who are isolated from the community and have many problems with which they would like to receive assistance. Unfortunately, the purposes of the study precluded the collection of data about the behavior and self-concepts of this group of blind people. Only one finding is suggestive in this regard. When Josephson asked respondents if they considered themselves to be blind, his analysis showed that the unaided were much more likely than the aided to report that they did not.[5] This finding may mean that only those who perceive themselves as blind are motivated to seek help from blindness agencies; it may mean that people who receive help from blindness agencies come to define themselves as blind because of this help; or it may indicate a person-

[2] Eric Josephson, *The Social Life of Blind People*, Research Series No. 19, American Foundation for the Blind, New York, 1968.

[3] *Ibid.*, pp. 71–72.

[4] *Ibid.*

[5] *Ibid.*, pp. 17–20.

ality characteristic relating to unwillingness to face a harsh reality. The question of which interpretation is more nearly correct is a critical one for the theory and practice of work for the blind.

THE INDEPENDENT BLIND

Of the blind people who have been clients and trainees of blindness organizations but are now living on their own in the community, some have returned to the jobs they originally held before losing their vision and others have secured similar types of competitive employment. Many have rejoined their original circle of friends and have assumed other roles they once played. These people are making a determined effort either to lead the kind of life that they led before becoming blind or (in the case of those who were blinded earlier in life) to become an integral part of the community.

No figures are available concerning the number of blind people who have been able to effect this type of adjustment. In all probability, it is quite small. Few agencies in the blindness field practice the kind of restorative approach to rehabilitation that trains a blind person to live independently. Furthermore, this form of independent adaptation to blindness depends upon more than just the type of rehabilitation training a blind person has received; he also needs a variety of personal resources and opportunities and a special kind of supportive relationship with friends, family members, employers, and other key people who affect his access to the community. There are, of course, few blind people who have these financial and social resources.

While it is not a necessary condition for independence, blind people who manage to live independent lives often have either an independent income or some special and unusual quality or talent, or both. For example, many independent blind people are excellent writers and musicians. These people seem to be able to "make it" in the sighted world because they have enough wealth, fame, or prestige to attract sighted people to them.[6]

[6] This observation, incidentally, provides some confirmation of the thesis I proposed concerning blindness as a form of social dependency. It suggests that sighted people are less resistant to engaging in contacts with blind people who are rich, talented, or famous, because the rewards from the affiliation compensate for the inconveniences.

Little information is available concerning the attitudes and be-havior of the independent blind. During the course of my study, I interviewed a half-dozen blind people in this category. In no case did I find evidence of the attitudes and behavior patterns so common among clients of agencies practicing the accommodative approach to rehabilitation. Indeed, no attitudes and behavior patterns relating to blindness were common to this group of independent blind people. These data are based on too small a sample to justify conclusions about all the independent blind, but they do at least suggest that the behavior and attitudes of the blind are not given by the condition but are learned in a variety of personal and organizational contexts.

One interview in particular provides anecdotal evidence on this point. The respondent was a very successful author and radio writer who became totally blind in his early adult life. At the time of his blindness, people with his skills were in very short supply, and his employer had promised him that he could continue in his job after he was rehabilitated. When he went to a large private blindness agency seeking rehabilitation services, his counselors discouraged him from planning a return to his job. They told him he was un-realistic and not adjusting to his blindness. He was offered employ-ment as a broom maker in the agency's sheltered workshop, and his rehabilitation regime consisted essentially of preparation for that position. Out of frustration, he finally left the organization and effec-tively rehabilitated himself. Following his return to competitive employment as a writer, he wrote a book that was highly critical of the whole blindness system. As his book became widely known, he came to know many blind people who were or had been clients of blindness agencies. He found that most of the behavior patterns and attitudes these people displayed as clients of blindness agencies were absent in his contacts with them. He told me: "But the one thing that happens is that [expressions of gratitude and helpless-ness] sure fall away and disappear from these people when they do not need them anymore." He went to observe of himself, "But certainly if I had to go to [name of a blindness agency], if this apartment were swept away from me and my bank account blew up, I would be a very well-behaved boy; a very well-behaved boy, don't you worry about that. You would hear me recant all over the

place. I would sound like one of the boys who was burning at the
stake in the 14th century. I would not only praise [name of agency],
I would compose music for them."

BLIND BEGGARS

Blind beggars represent an interesting, if somewhat unusual vari-
ant of the independent blind. These are persons who have broken
away from the blindness system in order to exploit for their own
economic gain the emotions and fears sighted people have about
blindness. Blind people who beg have usually received rehabilitation
and other services through one or more community agencies. Most
of the ones I spoke to had only a sporadic work history before
becoming blind, and a few of them had been chronically unemployed. These persons reject established blindness programs and set
out on their own as beggars. They are held in great disdain by almost
all workers for the blind and many blind people as well, who say
that they do great harm to the cause of bettering the position of
the blind in society because they exploit, and thereby reinforce,
stereotypic ideas about blindness.

To understand who blind beggars are and why they beg we must
first eliminate some common misconceptions about them. First, most
blind beggars are not unemployable. Quite the contrary, they are
usually able-bodied persons who are well suited for work either in
commercial industry or in sheltered workshops. Begging is hard work
and requires great stamina. A beggar is exposed to the elements for
long periods of time. He must be able to move about quite freely from
area to area as crowds subside or their generosity diminishes. Most
blind beggars in cities are able to use public transportation, which
many other blind people cannot. Most of them are able to keep their
composure in the midst of huge crowds, an ability shared by few
other blind people. We are, then, dealing with able-bodied blind
persons who prove themselves competent to perform independently
by the very conditions under which they beg.

Second, the "causes" to which contributors give are usually fictitious. It is common for the beggar to wear a sign explaining that he

or she needs money for a new guide dog or an eye operation that will restore vision. In fact, only under the most unusual conditions is it even possible for a blind person to purchase a guide dog. The schools in which training is given are usually endowed, nonprofit organizations that charge no fee or only a nominal fee for services. The notion of an eye operation is equally fictitious, since the visual problems of most blind beggars cannot be solved by surgery.

Third, many people incorrectly assume that the blind person has been driven to beg because of a lack of opportunity for retraining or because welfare cannot or will not sustain him. As we have noted, since beggars are among the heartiest of all blind persons, their capacity for retraining is good. In addition, many of the ones with whom I spoke were on welfare even though they were specifically enjoined not to beg as a precondition for receiving it. Thus, they are not begging because no other options exist or because they have no money.

Why, then, do some blind persons take to begging? One reason is that begging is lucrative. Most of the beggars to whom I spoke were able to earn more money this way than by working in a broom shop. A few of them make a substantial income by begging. Furthermore, begging is preferable to the kinds of jobs ordinarily available to them. Since most of them were not trained for the better jobs that blind persons can get, they could only hope for a small income doing highly routinized work in a broom shop. To these persons, begging is easier and less draining than performing routine, boring assembly work in a sheltered workshop. Third, most of them expressed bitterness at the patronizing attitudes of certain blindness workers and of the general public as well. They do not wish to give public testimonials in which they must express gratitude for the services they get. Their begging would seem to be inconsistent with this resentment, since it deliberately creates situations in which paternalism and pity are evoked. However, the psychological transactions between beggar and patron are exactly the opposite of what they seem to be. The beggar deliberately exploits the emotions of the sighted person by exaggerating key elements of the dependency role into which most persons would thrust him. He says, in effect, "I will be the helpless, pathetic person you ask me to be, but for this I demand payment." No matter what the consequences for other blind persons may be, it must be admitted that this is an extraordinarily effective psychological adaptation to blindness. The individual vents himself of the hostility he feels toward sighted persons by lucrative means.

Finally, blind persons beg because begging gives them much greater freedom than they would have as clients of agencies. No one tells them what to do, how to do it, or when to do it. They are very much their own bosses.

Obviously, it takes a special kind of person to become a beggar. Blind beggars probably come from marginal segments of the society where commitment to the mainstream of American values is not deep; in fact, such values may be scorned. They are consequently not as vulnerable to guilt or remorse for their deliberate manipulation and exploitation of the emotions of others.

It is essential to recognize that the causes of this adaptation to blindness lie not only in the psychology of marginal individuals but in general reactions to blindness as well. If sighted persons did not pity the blind, or cut them off from the mainstream of society, or force them into positions of helplessness, or patronize them, begging could not exist. There would be no motivation to beg, and there would be no market for the beggar's product. In this sense, judgments about the seemingly immoral actions of beggars are incongruent with the responses to and treatment of blind persons by the sighted.

BLINDED VETERANS

The final group of blind people outside institutions for the blind are blinded veterans of the armed forces of the United States. A great deal can be learned about the impact of existing intervention systems by comparing blinded veterans with the civilian blind. The range and breadth of services and benefits available to blinded veterans are different in several crucial ways from the services and benefits available to the civilian blind. Veterans with service-connected impairments are automatically granted financial benefits on the basis of the severity of the impairment and the circumstance under which it was incurred. No means test is required, nor is the amount of compensation in any other way related to income from other sources. The compensation is generous in comparison to the benefits paid through income-maintenance programs for the civilian blind. For example, blinded veterans with war-related, service-connected disabilities rated at 70 percent of total disability (70 percent disability is the equivalent of a visual acuity of 20/200) automatically receives $161 per month; a veteran who is totally visually disabled (defined as 5/200 vision) is entitled to receive $400 per month. If only light perception remains, this amount increases to $450, and when there is an anatomical loss of both eyes, a veteran is entitled to $500. According to a 1964 report by the Veterans' Administration, 2,358 veterans were receiving compensation for service-connected blindness, with an average monthly payment of $443.34. This figure excludes other financial benefits, such as dependency allowances, to which the veteran is also entitled. By contrast, the average payment to civilian blind who are recipients of Aid to the Needy Blind was about $87.[7]

These financial benefits give the blinded veteran a great deal more independence than the civilian blind are able to achieve from income-maintenance programs. Unlike civilian income-maintenance programs, the blinded veteran's benefits are unaffected by the amount of income he earns through employment. With a fairly high economic platform under him, the blinded veteran who is unable to work need not fear poverty. Those who are able to work can afford to exericse more discretion in selecting jobs and evaluating conditions of work. The amount of the benefits permit at least a reasonable standard of living and style of life, particularly when these benefits are supplemented with earned income. This system of income maintenance for the blind is the only one which genuinely facilitates independence.

A second service offered to blinded veterans by the Veterans' Administration is comprehensive rehabilitation. Like certain programs for the civilian blind, these services are based upon a restorative

[7] *Health, Education and Welfare Indicators*, January 1967.

approach to rehabilitation; they are aimed at providing a blinded veteran with the kind of skills that enable him to get about on his own in his home community. All veterans of the armed forces who become blind, regardless of whether their disability is service connected or not, are eligible for these services.

An important fact about this rehabilitation program is that its organization is set up in such a way that an accommodative approach is virtually impossible. Blinded veterans are sent to one of three special centers for rehabilitation with the understanding that they will remain there only for a predetermined, limited period of time. Their entire rehabilitation is geared to the assumption that they will be returning to their home communities. No provision is made in any of the rehabilitation centers for a blind person to remain in its care for a prolonged period of time. The only accommodative institutions within the structure of the Veterans' Adminstration are the domiciles connected to a few Veterans' Hospitals throughout the country. Only a small number of blinded veterans live in these domiciles; a majority return to their homes.

The income-maintenance program, the rehabilitation programs and the programs of other benefits provided by the Veterans' Administration are all aimed at helping the blind veteran attain a reasonable degree of independence.

The key question, of course, is the impact of these programs on their recipients. Fortunately, excellent data have been collected on this group of blind people. In a classic evaluative study, Graham and his colleagues obtained detailed data from a sample of 851 blinded veterans whose disabilities were service connected.[8] Data were obtained from interviews and examinations of blinded veterans who were known to eight of the regional Veterans' Administration Centers. The purpose of the study was to determine what these veterans were doing long after the onset of their blindness. In order to determine this, Graham and his colleagues obtained detailed information about work histories, educational attainments, family relationships, leisure-time activities, medical and mental health, social relationships, and participation in general community affairs. The in-

[8] Milton D. Graham *et al.*, *851 Blinded Veterans: A Success Story*, American Foundation for the Blind, New York, 1968.

vestigators concluded that there "are few, if any differences between [them] and the sighted male population of the same age groups."[9] After determining that their median age is close to that of the male veteran population of the United States, and that the distribution of nonwhites in the group is very nearly the same as it is in the national distribution, they found that about the same proportion of blinded veterans as non-disabled veterans in the population own their own homes. In terms of other factors, such as the number of people who are dependent upon them and their leisure-time activities, blinded veterans cannot be distinguished from the sighted male population of the same age in this country.[10]

There are however, certain positive respects in which they are different. It is worth quoting directly from the report about these differences:

(1) They are better educated; 45 percent took advantage of the GI Bill, about 20 percent in vocational training, 20 percent in college training, and 5 percent in secondary school academic training. (2) Their average family household income is higher—$8,600 versus the national average of $6,600. (3) Social workers concluded that the group is mostly positive in its handling of rehabilitation experiences, family situations, and relations with the community and in its general pattern of daily activities. (4) Their reports of health conditions that affect activity are fairly accurate, which could be interpreted as a realistic appraisal of activity-limiting conditions. (5) Clinical findings showed few anxiety or depression symptoms that clearly arise from their impairments or chronic conditions. (6) They read more, maybe twice as much as the general sighted population. The two-thirds of the group who are moderate to heavy readers are younger, more intelligent, better educated, and more active in organizations and have a higher self-image than the nonreaders. (7) They are gregarious; they visit a great deal more than it is estimated the general population does. (8) They also join more organizations (nonblind principally) than is estimated for the national population.[11]

There are also certain negative differences between this group of blind people and the general population. In certain respects, their

[9] *Ibid.*, p. 124.
[10] *Ibid.*
[11] *Ibid.*, pp. 124–125.

health is not so good; some of them appear to be more apathetic about their health than are sighted males; there is far more marital disruption in this group than in the average population; and fewer of them than their sighted counterparts work.[12]

On the few items of information about the civilian blind population that are comparable to these data on blinded veterans, we find that the civilian blind of the same age, even those who are receiving services from blindness agencies, fare very badly. The civilian blind are, of course, much poorer. Whereas 90 percent of the blinded veterans whom Graham studied receive more than $4,000, 75 percent of the civilian blind receive less than $4,000 annually. They are less active in non–blindness-related clubs and organizations than blinded veterans; they visit less; they have fewer sighted friends; they do not engage in social activities to the same degree; and they tend to be more isolated.

These data indicate in a very striking way how alternative approaches to rehabilitation can produce radically different socialization outcomes among blind people. Organizational systems that are constructed so as to discourage dependence in fact produce independent blind people; systems that foster dependency by creating accommodated environments produce blind people who cannot function outside of them. There is no more dramatic way than this to demonstrate just how important a factor in the making of blind men are the organized efforts of blindness workers and blindness agencies.

[12] *Ibid.*, pp. 126–127.

CHAPTER 8

Summary and Conclusions

*T*HE major thesis of this book has been that blindness is a learned social role. People whose vision fails will learn in two contexts the attitudes and behavior patterns that the blind are supposed to have, in their personal relationships with those with normal vision and in the organizations that exist to serve and to help blind people.

The relationships between sighted and blind men contribute to the socialization experiences of blind men in a number of ways. The misconceptions of the seeing about the nature of blindness and its impact upon personality and behavior are expressed as expectations of the blind person's behavior. When he encounters a sighted person, the blind man usually feels that he must act in the way expected of him. Few blind men can ignore the stereotypic beliefs held by the sighted. Some actually come to believe in these stereotypes themselves and internalize them; others insulate the self from them by various actions. In either case, the beliefs are a fact of life for people who are blind.

Blindness is also a condition that stigmatizes. The social identity of a man, indeed his whole personality, is spoiled when he is blinded. That he is regarded as a different and lesser person than others is sharply brought home to him whenever he has dealings with the sighted. A major component in the experience of being a blind man is defending the self from imputations of moral, psychological, and social inferiority. For some this defense succeeds and for others it fails, but for all blind men it is another fact of life.

Another set of socializing factors relates to the mechanics of dealing with someone who is blind. The norms that govern the conduct of the ordinary relationship of everyday life depend enormously on vision. When one of the actors in an encounter is blind, the situation is infused with ambiguity and uncertainty. Tensions arise over how to proceed, how to project a self-image, and how to evaluate the image projected by the other. The idiosyncratic responses of the seeing to this situation contribute to the blind man's socialization by reinforcing his conviction that he is different. Furthermore, his blindness denies him the honest, direct feedback essential to the development of a realistic self-concept.

Finally, because of the very nature of his condition, a blind man must rely on his sighted companions for assistance in the most ordinary situations, but he is restricted in his ability to reciprocate. Such encounters inevitably become relationships of social dependency. For all these reasons, blind people have difficulty establishing secure relationships with the sighted whom they regard as their intellectual and social equals. Here, again, the blind man is poignantly reminded that he is a different and lesser person than others.

Socialization processes that occur in the context of personal relationships are most salient for people readily identifiable as blind. Socialization processes that occur in blindness organizations could be salient for all persons who have been identified as blind according to the currently accepted administrative definition. Actually, only a highly selected segment of the blindness population is involved. My analysis shows that the blindness system, by which I mean the total network of agencies, organizations and programs for the blind, caters to about one-quarter of all people who are, according to administrative regulations, blind. These are the blind children who can be educated and the blind adults who can be employed. The system largely screens out the elderly, the unemployable, the uneducable, and the multiply-handicapped—in other words, the vast bulk of the blindness population.

When those who have been screened into blindness agencies enter them, they may not be able to see at all or they may have serious difficulties with their vision. When they have been rehabilitated, they are all blind men. They have learned the attitudes and behavior patterns that professional blindness workers believe blind people should have. In the intensive face-to-face relationships between blindness workers and clients that make up the rehabilitation process, the blind person is rewarded for adopting a view of himself that is consistent with his rehabilitators' view of him and punished for clinging to other self-conceptions. He is told that he is "insightful" when he comes to describe his problems and his personality as his rehabilitators view them, and he is said to be "blocking" or "resisting" when he does not. Indeed, passage through the blindness system is determined in part by his willingness to adopt the experts' views about self.

Gradually, over time, the behavior of blind men comes to correspond with the assumptions and beliefs that blindness workers hold about blindness, whether these beliefs follow the restorative or the accommodative approach. The restorative approach assumes that blind people can lead independent and fulfilled lives in the outside world, but only if they first recognize and accept as final the fact that they are blind. The accommodative approach regards these objectives as noble but unrealistic for most blind people. It holds that a more realistic objective is to provide environments to which blind people can accommodate with a minimum of effort. Such environments are created and sustained in many blindness agencies and in most sheltered workshops as well. Those of the blind who live in them can function well there, but in the process they become seriously maladjusted to the outside world.

Which of these approaches is adopted by a blindness agency depends only partly on the theoretical preferences of its blindness workers; it also depends on political, economic, and sociological pressures that arise inside and outside the agency. One such pressure is created by the unconscious desire of many persons in the community to avoid blind people by hiding them. Agencies that acquiesce to this pressure are rewarded with the generous donations of a grateful public. Another pressure is created because of the competition that often arises between blindness agencies in the same community for the comparatively small number of blind people in it who can benefit from the services they offer. An agency is reluctant to lose a client who can be educated or employed, because they may not be able to replace him. An accommodative approach to rehabilitation is thus insurance against potential drains in the client pool. Again, many blindness workers gain their status in the field of work for the blind through experience rather than through professional training. The expertise acquired through experience is closely linked to one agency and may not be transferrable to another. For this reason, any blindness worker who has not been professionally trained in a generic field develops a deeply vested interest in preserving the organization he works for. Whenever decisions must be made involving the interests of the agency, he has little choice but to opt for the policy that is best for the agency, even when it may be detrimental to the clients. Few blindness workers can afford to ignore the fact that the agency's fiscal integrity is more secure when an accommodative approach is adopted.

The overpowering importance of the blindness system in the socialization of the blind who are in it is demonstrated by looking at the blind who live outside it. These people, particularly blinded veterans and the independent blind, fail to display the attitudinal and behavioral patterns that so many insist they should have because they are blind. This demonstrates not only the importance of blindness organizations as agents of the socialization of the blind; it also demonstrates that blind men indeed are made.

The picture that emerges from my analysis is of a group of people who initially share in common only the fact that they have problems of vision and eventually come to feel and behave in patterned, predictable ways. People who initially think of themselves as sighted people who have trouble seeing come to think of themselves as blind people who have residual vision. Blindness becomes the primary factor around which they organize their lives and in terms of which they relate to other people. In this process, the role of organized helping efforts looms very large indeed.

My characterization of what this role of organized help involves would not be accepted by many blindness workers. They have tended to view blindness agencies, and the entire rehabilitation effort in our society, as an organized attempt, through strategic intervention, to divert the course of personality and social development presumably caused by blindness. My analysis suggests that such organizations *create* for blind people the experiences of being blind. Such organizations are not, as some have suggested, merely helpers of the blind that facilitate or change processes already occurring; rather, they are active socializing agents that create and mold the fundamental attitudes and patterns of behavior that are at the core of the experience of being a blind man.

Some may regard as deplorable the fact that blindness agencies have so great an impact upon the very nature of the phenomenon of blindness in our society. I do not, for it suggests that this system has the potential of becoming a powerful tool for positive social change. Indeed, were it otherwise, there would be a great deal more cause for concern. Blind men are not born, they are made; the challenge to an organized intervention system such as work for the blind is to render the process by which this occurs both rational and deliberate. The first step that must be taken in order to transform the current system from a tool with uncertain and unintended consequences for the blind it purportedly serves into one that can be used for positive change is to reexamine and critically evaluate the scientific validity of blindness workers' assumptions about blindness and the blind.

APPENDIX A

History of Work for the Blind

THE beginning of organized work for
the blind in America is usually set at 1828, the year in which the
Massachusetts legislature passed a bill incorporating the New England Asylum for the Blind.[1] Interest in establishing a school for the
blind had been stimulated by a Boston physician, Dr. John D. Fisher,
who, while touring Europe, visited a school for the blind in France.
Returning to Boston in 1826, he organized a committee, which applied to the legislature for an act of incorporation for a school for
the blind. Samuel Gridley Howe, a physician and social revolutionary, was appointed head of the Asylum (later called Perkins School
for the Blind), the doors of which opened to students in 1832. At
about the same time, other schools for blind children began to open
throughout the eastern part of the United States. New York

---

[1] Gabriel Farrell, "Blindness in the United States," in Paul A. Zahl, ed.,
Blindness: Modern Approaches to the Unseen Environment, Hafner Publishing Company, New York, 1962.

Institute for the Blind began to accept students in 1831, and a school
for the blind was begun in Philadelphia in 1833. Since Dr. Howe
was deeply interested in establishing a network of residential schools
for the blind throughout the country, he traveled to a number of
states to plead the cause of blind children before state legislatures.
As a result of his visits, residential schools were established in Ohio
(1837), Virginia (1840), South Carolina (1841), and Kentucky
(1842). Other states followed, and soon there were dozens of residential schools for the blind throughout the country.

As students were graduated from schools for the blind, they encountered great difficulty in obtaining employment. In an effort to
remedy this problem, residential schools began to build their own
workshops, in which they trained their graduates for industrial employment. Perkins opened a workshop in 1840; the New York Institute followed suit in 1845; six years later the school for the blind
in Philadelphia opened its workshop. In the states Howe visited
whose legislatures he had persuaded to open special schools, workshops began to operate under government auspices. In addition,
many other states that did not have residential schools began to support workshops and other special facilities for employing the blind.

State legislatures also began to take cognizance of the problem of
blind persons who could not work and who were in need of financial
aid. Laws were passed providing for public assistance in a number
of states, notably Indiana (1840), New York (1888), and Ohio
1898. Very quickly thereafter, the principle of special welfare
programs for the blind, financed by public funds, became firmly
established.

These three programs—residential schools, sheltered workshops,
and financial aid to the blind—began to grow in this country in the
middle of the nineteenth century. By 1900, organized work for the
blind was firmly established as a recognized specialty of social welfare in America.

It was not by chance that work for the blind became organized
when it did, nor can its growth be entirely explained, as historians
of the field have tried to do, by the extraordinary insights of one or
two unusual individuals. Such an explanation ignores a central fact

about work for the blind, that it is a product of the society that sustains it. Work for the blind was being organized at the same time that America was becoming industrialized. The social and physical environment of America was changing to such a degree that the problems blind persons faced were different from those they had faced in earlier times, and traditional ways of accommodating the blind were becoming impracticable. Gradually, an acute need developed for alternative ways of coping with the problems of blindness. Ironically, the development of organized work for the blind was made possible by the very social changes that had made traditional ways of dealing with the blind obsolete.

Four of the many changes in America occasioned by industrialization had special significance for the blind: the proliferation and growth of large cities; the development of occupational specialization, accompanying a complex division of labor; the decline of the extended family; and the increase in mechanization.[2]

THE URBAN ENVIRONMENT

The urban environment, in both its physical and social aspects, made organized services for the blind necessary. The physical environment of the city was cluttered, mechanized, and complicated. Heavy traffic, crowded streets and sidewalks, construction, and other hazards made negotiating city streets a serious matter for blind persons. Problems of mobility could no longer be solved by personal initiative or the intervention of friends; specialized training was required.

The quality of social relations differed considerably between urban and rural areas.[3] There was little difference in terms of intimacy among family members and friends, but the secondary relationships were different. In rural areas, most relationships were intrinsic, governed by personal characteristics; in cities, by far the greater proportion were extrinsic, governed by the positions people occupy. Social

[2] Harold L. Wilensky and Charles N. Lebeaux, *Industrial Society and Social Welfare*, Russell Sage Foundation, New York, 1958.

[3] Robert Bierstedt, *The Social Order*, McGraw-Hill Book Company, Inc., New York, 1957, Chap. 12.

relations in rural areas therefore had a quality of warmth and famil-
iarity in sharp contrast to the impersonal and circumscribed nature
of social relations in cities. This difference went even further. In
rural communities, the welfare of each member was felt to be the
responsibility of everyone in the community. In cities, the vast number of people and of extrinsic relationships precluded individual
responsibility for the plight of others. Individual responsibility was
replaced by welfare services. Community responsibility for socially
handicapped people, including the blind, was vested in secondary agencies. With the growth in number and size of cities came
a corresponding growth in the number and size of secondary
organizations.

Conditions of urban life created not only the necessity of organized services for the blind but the conditions for their implemen-
tation. Blindness is a relatively rare event in our society. In cities,
large numbers of blind persons were brought together for the first
time in history. The enormous financial resources available in the
city made organized welfare work for the blind economically
feasible.

Not only are there almost limitless ways in which a person can
earn a living in a city, but there is variety in recreational activities,
education, religion, and politics. Persons of every ethnic and racial
group in the world live in one city, and cultural traditions from virtually every society in the world can be found. The urban dweller,
because he lives with these sharp contrasts, is not committed to the
single view of the world that persons in rural areas have; the urban
dweller is more willing to accept alternatives and innovations. The
limitations of city life are man-made; the limitations of rural life
are imposed by nature. In rural areas, there is a strong belief that
things must stay as they are, since all things are given in nature, and
therefore by God. In urban areas, innovations flourish. The ideas
that a blind child could be educated or that a blind man could do
industrial work were, in their day, revolutionary. It was not by
chance, therefore, that the first agencies for the blind were founded
in cities, or that those who established them had the cosmopolitan
outlook of the urban dweller.

OCCUPATIONAL SPECIALIZATION

In the early years of industrial growth, the complex skills of crafts-
men were reduced to the simple, repetitive tasks of an assembly line.
With the proliferation and growth of factories, labor became increasingly specialized. When complex skills were reduced to the specialized but simple tasks of the assembly line, persons who had never
before been considered as sources of labor began to be recruited for
industrial positions. These persons included women, children, and
the handicapped. For the first time, the blind could be considered a
labor source. The importance of employment to the blind provided a
strong incentive to those concerned with the welfare of the blind to
organize programs in which blind persons could obtain the kind of
training they would need in order to get a job.

THE DECLINE OF THE EXTENDED FAMILY

The place of work is an industrialized society shifted from the
home to the large factory. In the home, all the members of a family,
including relatives, participated in the production of goods, whereas
in the factory only one family member was employed. Alone, a
worker could no longer earn enough to support anyone outside his
immediate family. The immediate, or nuclear, family, replaced the
large extended family as the primary form of family life. The nuclear family tended to be small, for two reasons. First, the period of
economic dependency of each child on his family lengthened as
more training became necessary for employment. Since this prolonged dependency was a drain on family income, a large family
hindered the aspirations of both parents and children to improve
their place in the community. Second, in pursuing a career it was
necessary for the wage earner to have the freedom to move from one
location to another in search of better job opportunities. A large family made it difficult for the breadwinner to move as often as he had
to in order to pursue his career successfully. The nuclear family was
reluctant to incur long-term obligations to others. Lasting commitments to parents or relatives mitigated against the family's freedom
to move quickly and with a minimum of personal loss.

The change in the form of the family from an extended to a nuclear group had a number of implications for the blind. A blind
person could seriously hamper a family's chances of improving its
social status. Blindness is stigmatized in our society, and this stigma
may be a hindrance to a family's acceptance into circles influential
in an area important to it.

A blind child might hinder the family's status aspirations in a
number of other ways. The extra costs involved in caring for a blind
child, coupled with the fact that blind children remain dependent
upon their families for longer periods of time than sighted children,
absorb large sums of money that might otherwise be spent edu-
cating other children or purchasing the material goods that are the
evidence of improved social standing. Moreover, high social status
in a community is in part contingent upon the ability of the children
to improve, or at least maintain, the social status of their parents.
The problems of blindness made it unlikely that the blind child could
obtain work commensurate with the status of his family.

When blindness struck an unmarried, widowed, or older person,
he could be cared for by an extended family without too much
trouble. In the nuclear family, however, it became impossible for a
married brother or sister to absorb a blind sibling into his family
without jeopardizing the life chances of everyone. If blindness struck
the breadwinner of the family, the life chances of every family member would be even more severely affected.

One group of persons especially hard hit by these changes was the
elderly. Children moved from their home communities one at a time
until the parents were left by themselves. If they became ill or
disabled, their children could not care for them without incurring
unusally high social and economic costs. Since life expectancy
increased with industrialization at the same time that the extended
family disappeared, this problem was especially serious. The relevance of this to work for the blind was that blindness is principally
a problem of old persons. The majority of blind persons lose their
sight after retirement age or when retirement is imminent.

Organized work for the blind grew out of a desire on the part of
the blind and of the community to minimize these problems for the

family. New specialized programs for the care of children, older persons, and others who were marginal to the nuclear family had to be developed.

MECHANIZATION

All of the changes we have discussed so far had a common effect on the increase in the amount of mechanization. The growth of cities and related organizational changes made necessary the development of mechanical devices in such fields as food processing, transportation, and communication.[4] The increase in the number of mechanical devices needed for meeting everyday needs created additional problems for the blind, because most of these devices were designed on the assumption that their users could see. Life became so enormously complicated for the blind person in a mechanical environment that specialized training was required before he could function. Increased mechanization therefore contributed to the need for organized services for the blind.

---

[4] Richard T. LaPiere, *Social Change*, McGraw-Hill Book Company, Inc., New York, 1965, Chap. 8.

The Relationship Between

Scientific Theory and

Practice Theory

ONE of the recurrent themes in this volume has been that the beliefs and assumptions of blindness workers about blind people have a profound impact upon blind people's experiences of their disability. In spite of this, many of these beliefs and assumptions remain implicit and unexamined. One implication of my analysis is that such beliefs must be made explicit, codified, and then critically examined in the light of scientific knowledge about human behavior and social processes. Only when this is done will such beliefs become tools for accomplishing desired social changes. The recurrent questions posed to me by blindness workers are: "How can this be done?" and "What will we have when this work is completed?" To answer these two questions, I must explain, first, the nature of scientific theory, then the nature of practice theory, and, finally, the connections that can be made between them.

Blindness workers have often told me that the facts about blindness are obvious and speak for themselves; that to introduce notions about scientific or practice theories will only confuse matters. They ask: "Of what possible value can theories be if the facts are already clear and the solutions obvious?" "Why waste time on armchair philosophies when so many concrete things need to be done?" One an-answer to these questions is that the "facts" of blindness are no more intuitively apparent than are the "facts" of any other disability, or of any other phenomenon, for that matter. What we perceive in a situation, and by the same token what we do not perceive in it, are both determined by the predispositions and definitions we bring to it. The facts of a situation are determined by how our precepts and concepts lead us to organize and integrate material. They do not inhere in the situation itself. Individuals agree on the facts of a situation only because they interpret the situation with the same concepts. In a majority of instances, of course, these shared concepts are implied and entirely unstated. At the same time, what constitutes a fact to one person is often only a part of the great unnoticed background for another. Any number of persons had observed an apple fall from a tree, but one, Sir Isaac Newton, was able to see it as a fact in a way that no one before him was able to do.

To say that the facts about blindness are obvious is only to say that persons share the same unstated frame of reference. To say that a theory is irrelevant to the hard practical activities of everyday life is to ignore the fact that what is hard and practical is determined by the concepts we use and the assumptions we make. For this reason, the idea that theory is something only for "higher-ups" and not for the rank and file, that it is something which interprets and explains, but does not determine, a program, is a misconception.

The existing body of ideas called "the theory of work for the blind" should be replaced with a meaningful set of concepts based upon scientific knowledge about human behavior. This set of concepts, which I will call the "practice theory of work for the blind," should *determine* and not merely *interpret* the nature and content of practice programs.[1] A meaningful practice theory is based on knowledge from the social and physical sciences that is appropriate to the prob-

[1] Ernest Greenwood, "Social Science and Social Work: A Theory of Their Relationship," *Social Science Review*, Vol. 29, No. 1, 1955, pp. 20–33.

lem areas of the practice theory. It is therefore impossible to discuss practice theory without also mentioning scientific theory. Since one of the purposes of this book is to determine the contribution of social science knowledge to work for the blind, I will limit my discussion to the social sciences, although biology, physics, and chemistry also have a clear relevance for the problems of the blind.

One of the principal goals of a science is to make generalizations about the objects of its study. The scientist attempts to identify uniformities that underlie events and objects of the real world. When uniformities are identified, the scientist uses them as the criteria for constructing logical classifications. He then observes the patterns of behavior among persons or groups in the classes he has identified, and from his observations he develops generalizations that explain what he has observed.

The aim of generalization applies not only to specific classes; the scientist also attempts to find similarities between events falling into different groupings in his system of classification. Thus, he not only attempts to formulate descriptive generalizations about all events that fall into class A; he also attempts to make generalizations that encompass A, B, C. Naturally, generalizations among classes are much wider and more abstract than those within classes. Generalizations among classes are called "scientific laws." It is possible to make even more abstract generalizations by relating different laws to one another. Ultimately, through this complex process of abstracting, comparing, and generalizing, a network of interrelated propositions emerges. These propositions, and all that they imply in the way of explanation and elaboration, constitute scientific theory.

Two processes are essential to the development of a body of theory: rigorous logic and empirical observation. Unless the scientist tests his generalizations against concrete events in the real world, his theory will be meaningless. At the same time, the failure to apply the canons of logic to his observations may result in meaningless observations and/or misinterpretation of empirical findings. The theory that emerges from this process represents the scientist's conception of the order that is believed to operate beneath the apparent confusion of events. This theory must be tested constantly in order to determine if it actually explains the events it purports to explain.

Observation is a critical aspect of theory building. The procedures and methods of observation cannot, therefore, be left to the whims and fancies of the individual observer. Instead, the procedures for scientific observation are formalized into a separate process that is called "research." Scientific research consists of a series of technical and logical procedures employed to test the empirical validity of theoretical formulations. The scientist, using deductive logic, formulates a hypothesis from a body of theory. He then selects a group of events in the real world on which to make observations that will test his hypothesis. The observations are collected by means of instruments that he devises. The group of events he selects for observation and the instruments he uses constitute the study design. When observations are made, he interprets them in terms of hypothesis. If the data support the hypothesis, the theory from which it was derived is verified; if the data do not support the hypothesis, then the theory must be modified to fit the findings. In order for research to be scientific, it must proceed from a body of theory and, in turn, it must be related back to that theory. Its goal is always to test and to expand scientific theory.

The scientist brings to this process certain attitudes that are important in helping him to determine the validity of his knowledge. He attempts to be as objective as he can when making observations; he avoids making moral and emotional commitments to the issues he studies in order to prevent his personal feelings from influencing his observations. He never accepts a theoretical formulation as final, only as tentative. He recognizes that theory must change in order to fit the facts. His interest in obtaining valid knowledge leads him to be skeptical; he questions all findings until their validity is established beyond the shadow of a doubt.

The social sciences have a body of theory that is rudimentary when compared to the theories of advanced sciences such physics and chemistry. Nevertheless, there is some empirically validated knowledge about human behavior and group process that has clear relevance for a practice theory of blindness. The first step in the process of applying this knowledge to the problems of blindness is for the social scientist to classify blindness as an instance of a class of phenomena he has already identified. Since the problems of blindness are multiple and complex, social science knowledge regarding sensory deprivation, social deviance, social roles, social interaction, socialization, and other classes of phenomena are all relevant. The generalizations that have been made about each of these phenomena can be applied to the problems of blindness. By this process, the problems of blindness can be conceptualized in a broader and essentially different way. New conceptualizations of the problem imply new solutions of it, solutions that can be empirically tested. Solutions that are successful can serve as the basis for developing action-oriented propositions about particular problems of blindness. Whenever these problems are observed in any particular instance of blindness, the generalized proposition can serve as a guide for corrective action. Generalized propositions that are based upon scientific knowledge of the social sciences are termed the "principles" of practice theory. The link between scientific theory and practice theory is, therefore, the transformation of scientific laws into principles of practice.

Principles based upon scientific generalizations are the cornerstone of practice theory. In order to understand how practice theory can operate in work for the blind, it will be helpful to consider, in a generic way, the nature of work for the blind. While there is some disagreement about the exact nature of this field, one thing about it is clear: work for the blind is a technology and not a science. Greenwood defines a technology as a discipline that aims "to achieve controlled changes in natural relationships by means of procedures that are scientifically based." The fact that work for the blind is committed to action and change points up the distinction between a practice field and a science. One of the principal goals of the social sciences is to amass accurate knowledge about human behavior and group processes; the principal goal of work for the blind is *control* of

² Ernest Greenwood, *The Practice of Science and the Science of Practice*, Brandeis University, Florence Heller Graduate School for Advanced Studies in Social Welfare, Papers in Social Welfare, No. 1, Waltham, Mass., 1960, p. 2.

human behavior and group processes. To the scientist, control is secondary to knowledge; to the practitioner, knowledge is secondary to control. Workers for the blind must intervene in situations in order to change them in desired directions. This points up one of the central facts about the transformation of scientific knowledge into practice principles: the transformation involves the introduction of a value component to knowledge that is essentially value-free.

Control of a situation is achieved through two fundamental processes: diagnosis and treatment. When we say that a diagnosis has been made, we imply a two-step process (1) we have knowledge about a situation that is defined as a problem, and (2) we use this knowledge to place the problem situation into a typology. A typology is definied by Greenwood as a "classification scheme, in which each type represents a constellation of factors."[3] The typology provides a way of differentiating between types of problems and of interpreting the features associated with them. It is desirable to amass sufficient information about each type of problem so that it becomes possible to develop generalizations about it.

In order to achieve his goal of controlled change, the practitioner must have knowledge of the features common to types, and he must also understand how each particular problem situation is different from all others. The practitioner is therefore concerned not only with similarities but with differences among problem situations. He uses the principles of diagnosis to help him discover the facts of the problem situation confronting him. As he learns more and more about it, he begins to compare the cluster of factors to those associated with the categories of his diagnostic typology. A diagnosis is made when he can positively show the similarity between the specific instance he examines and a particular category of typology.

Diagnosis of a problem is only half the task of the practitioner. The matter of treatment remains. The discipline should have a typology of treatment procedures that correspond to the diagnostic categories. This typology would include principles of treatment for each category, including stages of the treatment process, criteria for

[3] *Ibid.*, p. 11.

determining the appropriateness of each palliative effort, and a specification of how to measure success and failure. The effectiveness of the treatment is usually the criterion for measuring the accuracy of the diagnosis.

The practice theory of an applied discipline such as work for the blind should consist, therefore, of the description of the diagnostic and treatment typologies, in all their ramifications, implications, and rationalizations.[4] Practice theory is not scientific theory, but it must be based upon valid scientific knowledge; it is not value-free, but it must use value-free knowledge to formulate the principles of practice.

The place of research in practice theory should be clarified. Research enters into the process at three different points. First, it is through research that one can measure most accurately how effective and meaningful a diagnostic and treatment typology really is. Through continuing studies in practice settings, reliable information can be obtained about the effect of intervention upon the problem situation. Second, applied research can help to speed the process of amassing reliable information upon which principles of diagnosis and treatment are based. Third, research can be of value in refining and elaborating diagnostic and treatment categories by providing more detailed information about each category of a typology than could be obtained through informal observation.

Scientific research also makes an important contribution to practice by contributing to the development and elaboration of existing scientific knowledge about classes of phenomena of which blindness is an instance. This fact is often overlooked by the practitioner, who insists on supporting only research studies that have clear relevance for the problem that concerns him. It is the rare practitioner who is insightful enough to recognize that the support of scientific research for its own sake will yield new information of incalculable value in helping workers for the blind to solve the problems of the blind.

Three key processes must be built into an attempt to construct a

[4] *Ibid.*

practice theory of work for the blind if it is to make any meaningful contribution toward solving the problem: translation of all relevant scientific knowledge into principles of practice; codification of all knowledge about the problems of blindness into principles of diagnosis and treatment; constant evaluation of the effectiveness of practice theory through research into the impact of intervention upon a problem situation.

At the present time, much of the theory in work for the blind consists of ideas developed by trial and error which have never been subjected to meaningful empirical validation and which justify rather than determine the nature of intervention into a blind person's life in order to help him solve his problems. As a first step toward the development of meaningful practice theory in work for the blind, it is suggested that the scientific validity of the beliefs of workers for the blind be critically assessed.

BIBLIOGRAPHY

"An Analysis of Blindness and Services to the Blind in the United States," Organization for Social and Technical Innovation, Boston, 1967 mimeographed.

Annual Report, American Printing House for the Blind, Louisville, Ky., 1965.

Barker, Roger G., *et al., Adjustment to Physical Handicap and Illness: A Survey of the Social Psychology of Physique and Disability,* Social Science Research Council, New York, 1953.

Becker, Howard S., *Outsiders: Studies in the Sociology of Deviance,* The Free Press of Glencoe, New York, 1963.

Best, Harry, *Blindness and the Blind in the United States,* The Macmillan Company, New York, 1934.

Bierstedt, Robert, *The Social Order,* McGraw-Hill Book Company, Inc., New York, 1957.

Binocular Visual Acuity of Adults, United States, 1960–1962, U.S. Public Health Service, Washington, D.C., Series 11, No. 3, 1964.

Blank, H. Robert, "Psychoanalysis and Blindness," *Psychoanalytic Quarterly,* Vol. 26, No. 1, 1957, pp. 1–24.

Blau, Peter M., *Exchange and Power in Social Life,* John Wiley & Sons, Inc., New York, 1964.

Brim, Orville G., Jr., and Stanton Wheeler, *Socialization after Childhood,* John Wiley & Sons, Inc., New York, 1967.

Carroll, Thomas J., *Blindness: What It Is, What It Does, and How to Live with It,* Little, Brown and Company, Boston, 1961.

Characteristics of Patients in Mental Hospitals, United States, April-June, 1963, National Center for Health Statistics, Washington, D.C., Series 12, No. 3, 1965.

Characteristics of Residents in Institutions for the Aged and Chronically Ill, April-June, 1963, National Center for Health Statistics, Washington, D.C., 1965.

Chevigny, Hector, and Sydell Braverman, *The Adjustment of the Blind,* Yale University Press, New Haven, 1950.

Cholden, Louis A., *A Psychiatrist Works with Blindness,* American Foundation for the Blind, New York, 1958.

_____, "Some Psychiatric Problems in the Rehabilitation of the Blind," *Bulletin of the Menninger Clinic,* Vol. 18, No. 3, 1954, pp. 107–112.

Comparison of Two Vision-Testing Devices, National Center for Health Statistics, Washington, D.C., Series 2, No. 1, 1963.

Cutsforth, Thomas D., *The Blind in School and Society: A Psychological Study,* American Foundation for the Blind, New York, 1951.

Davis, Fred, "Deviance Disavowal: The Management of Strained Interaction by the Visibly Handicapped," in Howard S. Becker, ed., *The Other Side,* The Free Press of Glencoe, New York, 1964, pp. 119–138.

Directory of Agencies Serving Blind Persons in the United States, 15th ed., American Foundation for the Blind, New York, 1967.

Facts and Figures about Blindness, American Foundation for the Blind, New York, 1967.

Farrell, Gabriel, "Blindness in the United States," in Paul A. Zahl, ed., *Blindness: Modern Approaches to the Unseen Environment,* Hafner Publishing Company, New York, 1962.

Goffman, Erving, *Asylums,* Doubleday & Company, Inc., New York, 1961.

_____, *Stigma: Notes on the Management of Spoiled Identity,* Prentice-Hall, Inc., Englewood Cliffs, N.J., 1963.

Gowman, Alan G., "Blindness and the Role of the Companion," *Social Problems,* Vol. 4, No. 1, 1956, pp. 68–75.

_____, *The War Blind in American Social Structure,* American Foundation for the Blind, New York, 1957.

Graham, Milton D., *Multiply Impaired Blind Children: A National Problem,* American Foundation for the Blind, New York, 1968.

_____, "Toward a Functional Definition of Blindness," *Research Bulletin,* American Foundation for the Blind, New York, No. 3, 1963, pp. 130–133.

_____, *et al., 851 Blinded Veterans: A Success Story,* American Foundation for the Blind, New York, 1968.

Greenwood, Ernest, *The Practice of Science and the Science of Practice,* Brandeis University, Florence Heller Graduate School for Advanced Studies in Social Welfare, Papers in Social Welfare, No. 1, Waltham, Mass., 1960.

————, "Social Science and Social Work: A Theory of Their Relationship," *Social Science Review*, Vol. 29, No. 1, 1955, pp. 20–33.

Health, Education and Welfare Indicators, October 1966, January 1967.

Himes, Joseph S., "Some Concepts of Blindness in American Culture," *Social Casework*, Vol. 31, No. 10, 1950, pp. 410–416.

Homans, George C., *Social Behavior*, Harcourt, Brace & World, New York, 1961.

Home Teachers of the Adult Blind: What They Do; What They Could Do; What Will Enable Them to Do It, American Association of Workers for the Blind, Inc., Washington, D.C., 1961.

Hoover, Richard E., "Visual Efficieny as a Criterion of Service Needs," *Research Bulletin*, American Foundation for the Blind, New York, No. 3, 1963, pp. 116–119.

Hurlin, Ralph G., "Estimated Prevalence of Blindness in the United States," *Social Security Bulletin*, Vol. 8, No. 3, 1945, pp. 17–22.

————, "Estimated Prevalence of Blindness in the United States," *New Outlook for the Blind*, Vol. 47, No. 7, 1953, pp. 189–196.

————, "Estimated Prevalence of Blindness in the United States and in Individual States, 1960," *Sight-Saving Review*, Vol. 32, No. 1, 1962.

Impairments by Type, Sex and Age: United States, July 1957–June 1958, U.S. Public Health Service, Washington, D.C., Series B9, 1959.

Information Bulletin No. 59, University of Utah, Regional Rehabilitation Research Institute, Salt Lake City, 1968.

Josephson, Eric, *The Social Life of Blind People*, Research Series No. 19, American Foundation for the Blind, New York, 1968.

————, and Marvin B. Sussman, "A Pilot Study of Visual Impairment," American Foundation for the Blind, New York, 1965, mimeographed.

Kleck, Robert, Ono Hiroshi, and Albert H. Hastorf, "The Effects of Physical Deviance upon Face-to-Face Interaction," *Human Relations*, Vol. 19, No. 4, 1966, pp. 425–436.

LaPiere, Richard T., *Social Change*, McGraw-Hill Book Company, Inc., New York, 1965.

Lukoff, Irving F., and Martin Whiteman, "Attitudes and Blindness: Components, Correlates and Effects," Washington, D.C., 1963, mimeographed.

Mead, George H., *Mind, Self and Society*, ed. by Charles W. Morris, University of Chicago Press, Chicago, 1940.

The Model Reporting Area for Blindness Statistics, National Institute of Neurological Diseases and Blindness, Washington, D.C., 1966.

Mugge, Robert H., "Recipients of Aid to the Blind," *Welfare in Review,* April 1965.

Paske, Victor, and Walter Weiss, "Fitidsun Der Sogelsen," Copenhagen, 1965, mimeographed.

Richardson, Stephen A., "The Effects of Physical Disability on the Socialization of a Child," in David A. Goslin, ed., *Handbook of Socialization Theory and Research,* Rand McNally & Company, Chicago, 1969.

Scott, Robert A., "The Selection of Clients by Social Welfare Agencies: The Case of the Blind," *Social Problems,* Vol. 14, No. 3, 1967, pp. 248–257.

————, "The Socialization of the Blind Child," in David A. Goslin, ed., *Handbook of Socialization Theory and Research,* Rand McNally & Company, Chicago, 1969.

Selected Impairments by Etiology and Activity Limitation: United States, July 1959–June 1961, U. S. Public Health Service, Washington, D.C., Series B, No. 35, 1962.

Simmons, William D., "A Survey of Blind, Severely Visually Impaired, and Multiply-Handicapped Children in California: A Preliminary Report," *Proceedings of the West Coast Regional Conference on Research Related to Blind and Severely Visually Impaired Children,* American Foundation for the Blind, New York, 1965, pp. 11–15.

Snellen, Herman, *Test-Types for the Determination of the Acuteness of Vision,* Utrecht, 1868.

Wilensky, Harold L., and Charles N. Lebeaux, *Industrial Society and Social Welfare,* Russell Sage Foundation, New York, 1958.

INDEX